UNITED
THE COMIC STRIP HISTORY

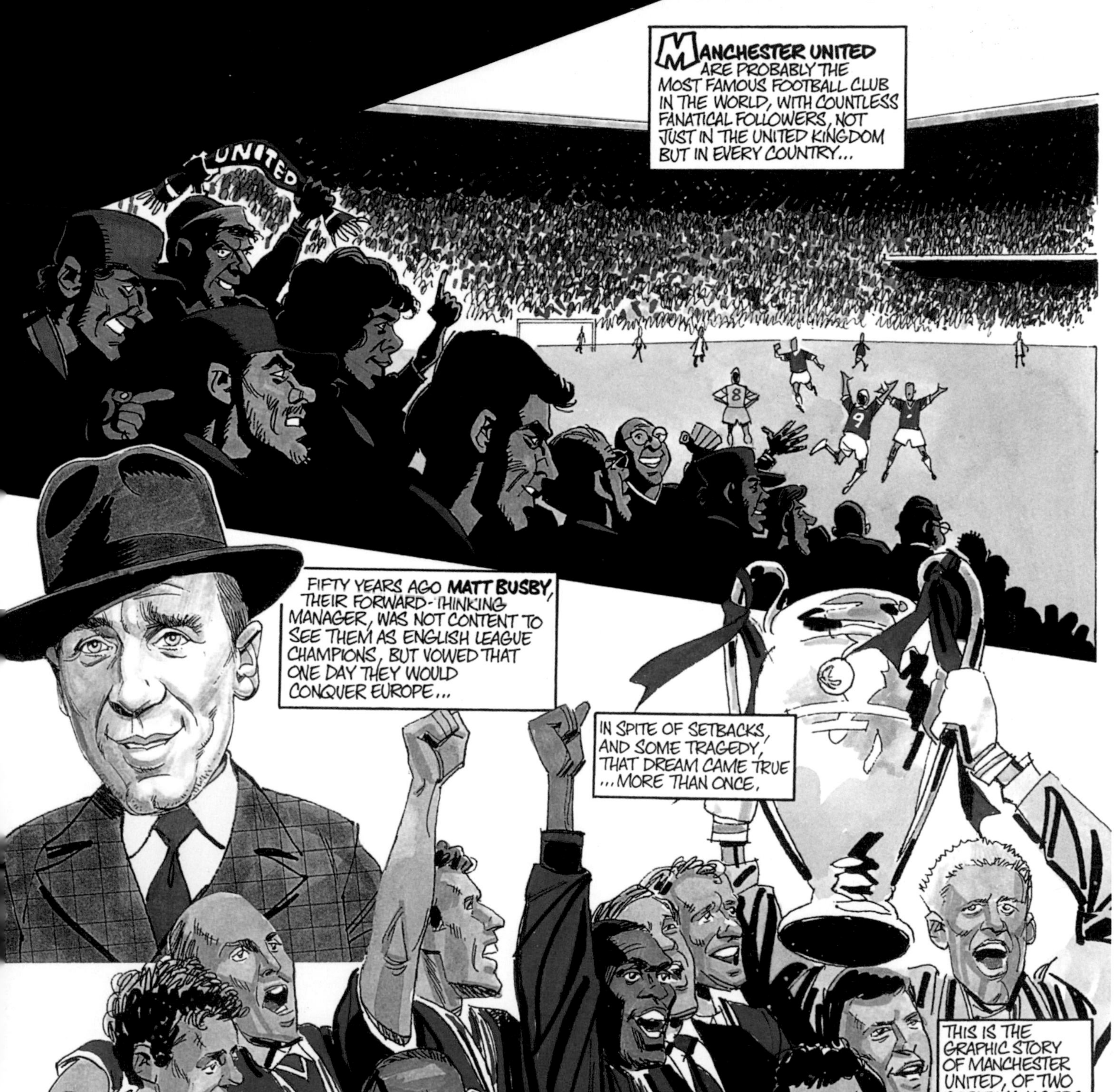
MANCHESTER UNITED ARE PROBABLY THE MOST FAMOUS FOOTBALL CLUB IN THE WORLD, WITH COUNTLESS FANATICAL FOLLOWERS, NOT JUST IN THE UNITED KINGDOM BUT IN EVERY COUNTRY...
UNITED
FIFTY YEARS AGO MATT BUSBY, THEIR FORWARD-THINKING MANAGER, WAS NOT CONTENT TO SEE THEM AS ENGLISH LEAGUE CHAMPIONS, BUT VOWED THAT ONE DAY THEY WOULD CONQUER EUROPE...
IN SPITE OF SETBACKS, AND SOME TRAGEDY, THAT DREAM CAME TRUE ...MORE THAN ONCE.
THIS IS THE GRAPHIC STORY OF MANCHESTER UNITED, OF TWO GREAT MANAGERS, OF WONDERFUL PLAYERS, AND OF MANY MEMORABLE ACHIEVEMENTS...

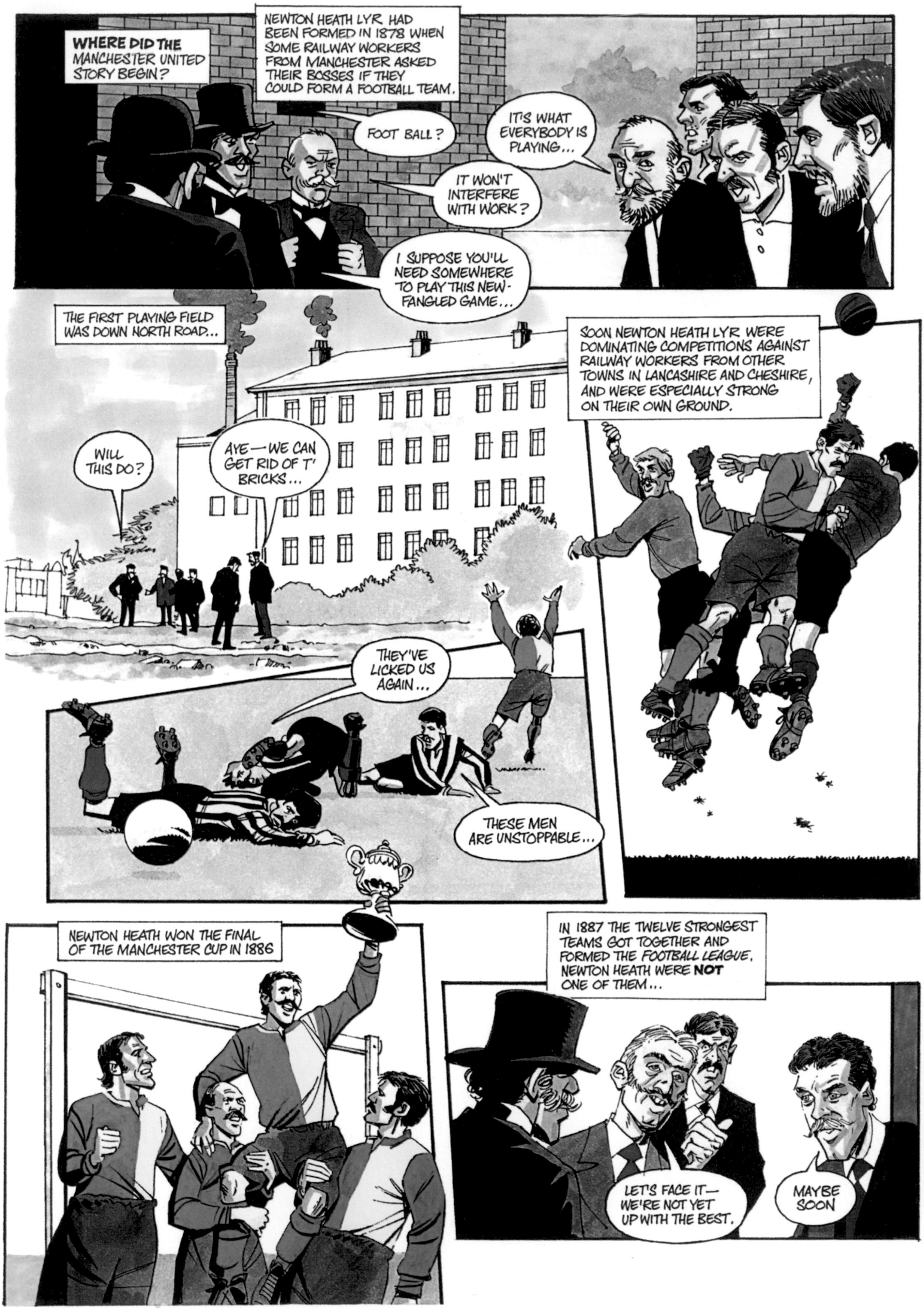
WHERE DID THE MANCHESTER UNITED STORY BEGIN?
NEWTON HEATH LYR HAD BEEN FORMED IN 1878 WHEN SOME RAILWAY WORKERS FROM MANCHESTER ASKED THEIR BOSSES IF THEY COULD FORM A FOOTBALL TEAM.
FOOT BALL?
IT'S WHAT EVERYBODY IS PLAYING...
IT WON'T INTERFERE WITH WORK?
I SUPPOSE YOU'LL NEED SOMEWHERE TO PLAY THIS NEW-FANGLED GAME...
THE FIRST PLAYING FIELD WAS DOWN NORTH ROAD...
WILL THIS DO?
AYE—WE CAN GET RID OF T' BRICKS...
SOON NEWTON HEATH LYR WERE DOMINATING COMPETITIONS AGAINST RAILWAY WORKERS FROM OTHER TOWNS IN LANCASHIRE AND CHESHIRE, AND WERE ESPECIALLY STRONG ON THEIR OWN GROUND.
THEY'VE LICKED US AGAIN...
THESE MEN ARE UNSTOPPABLE...
NEWTON HEATH WON THE FINAL OF THE MANCHESTER CUP IN 1886
IN 1887 THE TWELVE STRONGEST TEAMS GOT TOGETHER AND FORMED THE FOOTBALL LEAGUE. NEWTON HEATH WERE NOT ONE OF THEM...
LET'S FACE IT—WE'RE NOT YET UP WITH THE BEST.
MAYBE SOON

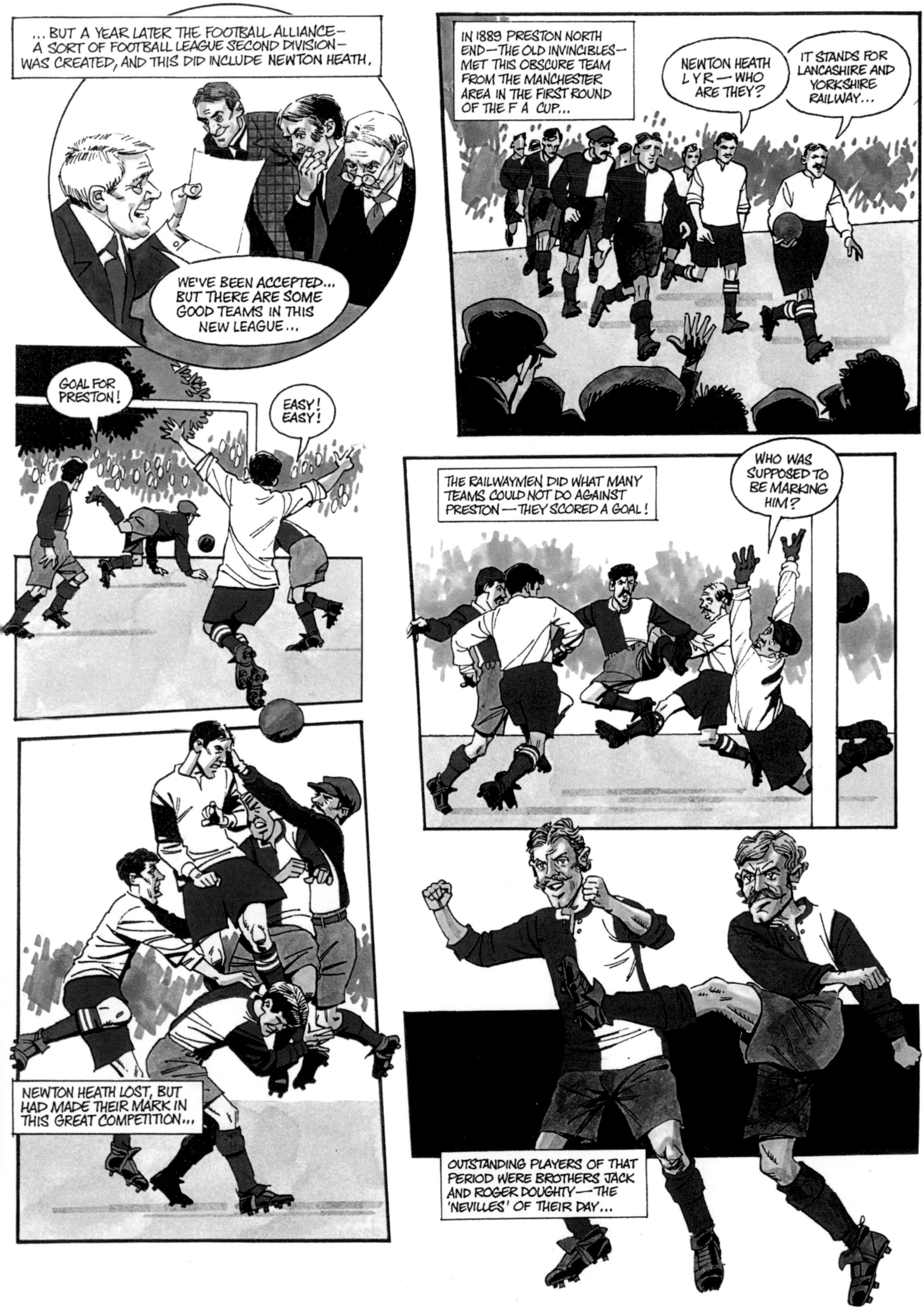

... BUT A YEAR LATER THE FOOTBALL ALLIANCE– A SORT OF FOOTBALL LEAGUE SECOND DIVISION– WAS CREATED, AND THIS DID INCLUDE NEWTON HEATH.
WE'VE BEEN ACCEPTED... BUT THERE ARE SOME GOOD TEAMS IN THIS NEW LEAGUE...
IN 1889 PRESTON NORTH END—THE OLD INVINCIBLES—MET THIS OBSCURE TEAM FROM THE MANCHESTER AREA IN THE FIRST ROUND OF THE F A CUP...
NEWTON HEATH L Y R — WHO ARE THEY?
IT STANDS FOR LANCASHIRE AND YORKSHIRE RAILWAY...
GOAL FOR PRESTON!
EASY! EASY!
THE RAILWAYMEN DID WHAT MANY TEAMS COULD NOT DO AGAINST PRESTON — THEY SCORED A GOAL!
WHO WAS SUPPOSED TO BE MARKING HIM?
NEWTON HEATH LOST, BUT HAD MADE THEIR MARK IN THIS GREAT COMPETITION...
OUTSTANDING PLAYERS OF THAT PERIOD WERE BROTHERS JACK AND ROGER DOUGHTY— THE 'NEVILLES' OF THEIR DAY...

THE FOOTBALL ALLIANCE ALSO INCLUDED A TEAM CALLED ARDWICK, WHO PLAYED NEWTON HEATH FOR THE FIRST TIME ON THE IMPREGNABLE NORTH ROAD PITCH...

...A SIGNIFICANT MEETING, BECAUSE NEWTON HEATH WOULD LATER BECOME MANCHESTER UNITED, AND ARDWICK CHANGED THEIR NAME TO MANCHESTER CITY...

IN 1892 NEWTON HEATH JOINED THE ELITE OF THE FIRST DIVISION, AND A YEAR LATER MOVED TO A NEW GROUND AT CLAYTON,

SMILE PLEASE INSIDE-LEFT... AND WATCH THE BIRDIE!

BUT SUCCESS AT THE VERY TOP DID NOT COME STRAIGHT AWAY. THEY COULD NOT COMPETE EASILY WITH TEAMS LIKE ASTON VILLA, EVERTON AND PRESTON.

COME ON, HEATHENS! YOU'RE ONLY THREE DOWN...

BOO! RUBBISH! BOOO BOO!

IN 1894 THEY WERE RELEGATED...

AFTER TEN VERY ORDINARY YEARS NEWTON HEATH WERE BACK IN DIVISION TWO, AND ON THE EDGE OF BANKRUPTCY WHEN CLUB CAPTAIN HARRY STAFFORD AND FOUR BUSINESSMEN STEPPED IN WITH A RESCUE PACKAGE...

WE MUST NO LONGER GO ON CALLING OURSELVES NEWTON HEATH.

WE NEED A NEW NAME...

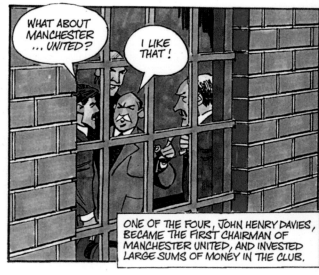

WHAT ABOUT MANCHESTER ... UNITED?

I LIKE THAT!

ONE OF THE FOUR, JOHN HENRY DAVIES, BECAME THE FIRST CHAIRMAN OF MANCHESTER UNITED, AND INVESTED LARGE SUMS OF MONEY IN THE CLUB.

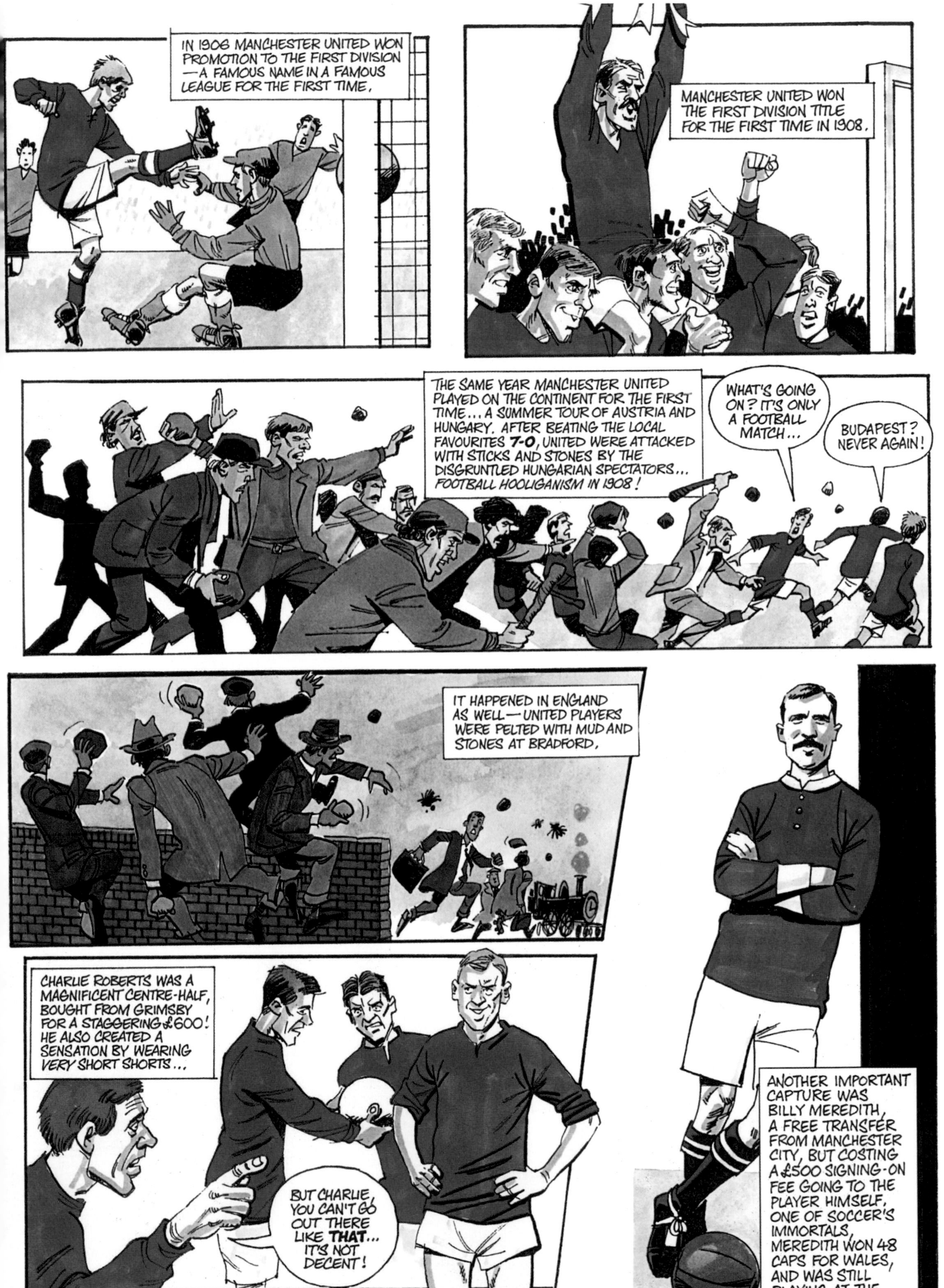
IN 1906 MANCHESTER UNITED WON PROMOTION TO THE FIRST DIVISION —A FAMOUS NAME IN A FAMOUS LEAGUE FOR THE FIRST TIME.
MANCHESTER UNITED WON THE FIRST DIVISION TITLE FOR THE FIRST TIME IN 1908.
THE SAME YEAR MANCHESTER UNITED PLAYED ON THE CONTINENT FOR THE FIRST TIME... A SUMMER TOUR OF AUSTRIA AND HUNGARY. AFTER BEATING THE LOCAL FAVOURITES **7-0**, UNITED WERE ATTACKED WITH STICKS AND STONES BY THE DISGRUNTLED HUNGARIAN SPECTATORS... *FOOTBALL HOOLIGANISM IN 1908!*
WHAT'S GOING ON? IT'S ONLY A FOOTBALL MATCH...
BUDAPEST? NEVER AGAIN!
IT HAPPENED IN ENGLAND AS WELL—UNITED PLAYERS WERE PELTED WITH MUD AND STONES AT BRADFORD.
CHARLIE ROBERTS WAS A MAGNIFICENT CENTRE-HALF, BOUGHT FROM GRIMSBY FOR A STAGGERING £600! HE ALSO CREATED A SENSATION BY WEARING *VERY SHORT SHORTS...*
BUT CHARLIE, YOU CAN'T GO OUT THERE LIKE **THAT**... IT'S NOT DECENT!
ANOTHER IMPORTANT CAPTURE WAS BILLY MEREDITH, A FREE TRANSFER FROM MANCHESTER CITY, BUT COSTING A £500 SIGNING-ON FEE GOING TO THE PLAYER HIMSELF. ONE OF SOCCER'S IMMORTALS, MEREDITH WON 48 CAPS FOR WALES, AND WAS STILL PLAYING AT THE AGE OF 51...

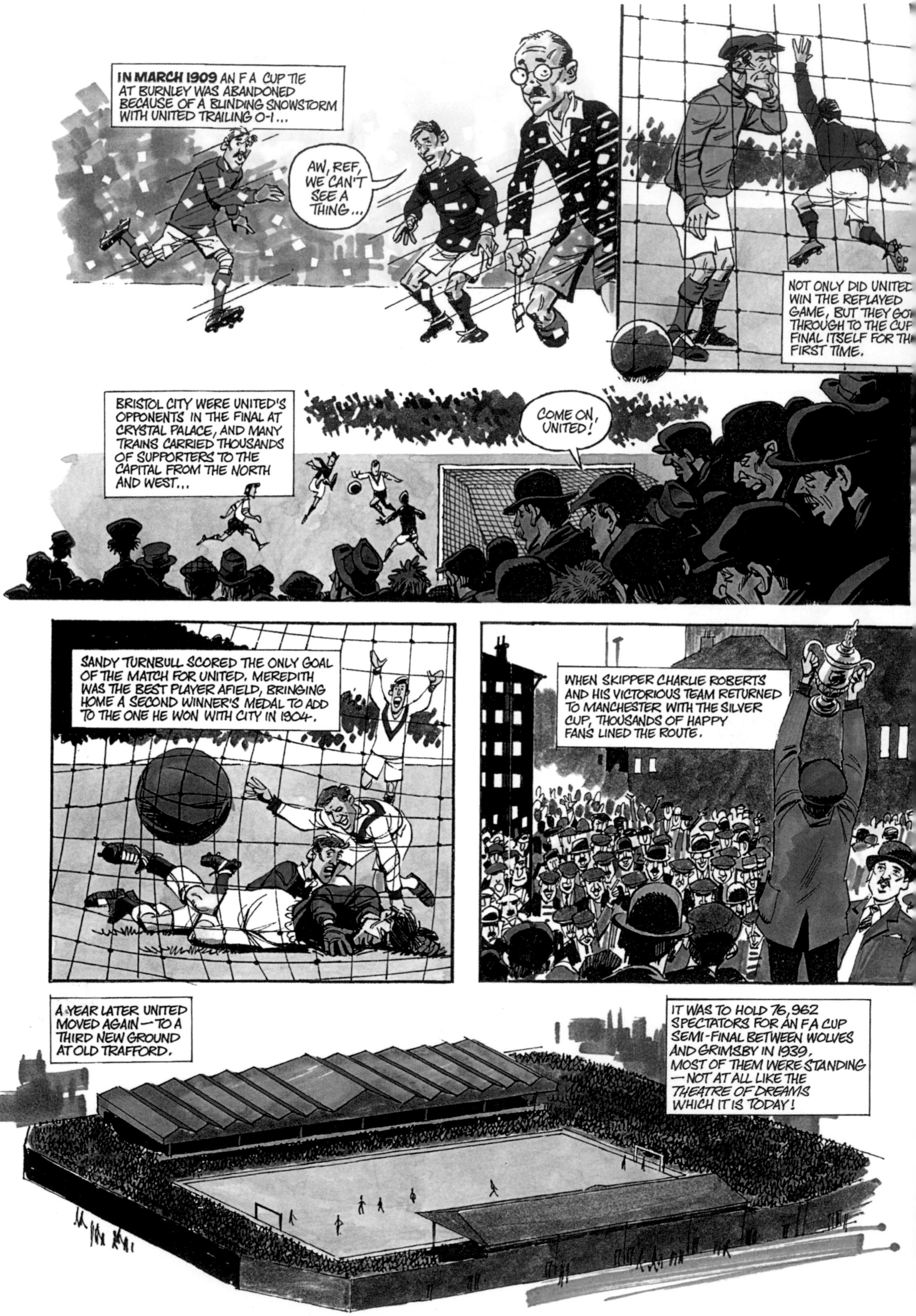
IN MARCH 1909 AN F A CUP TIE AT BURNLEY WAS ABANDONED BECAUSE OF A BLINDING SNOWSTORM WITH UNITED TRAILING 0-1...
AW, REF, WE CAN'T SEE A THING...
NOT ONLY DID UNITED WIN THE REPLAYED GAME, BUT THEY GO THROUGH TO THE CUP FINAL ITSELF FOR TH FIRST TIME.
BRISTOL CITY WERE UNITED'S OPPONENTS IN THE FINAL AT CRYSTAL PALACE, AND MANY TRAINS CARRIED THOUSANDS OF SUPPORTERS TO THE CAPITAL FROM THE NORTH AND WEST...
COME ON, UNITED!
SANDY TURNBULL SCORED THE ONLY GOAL OF THE MATCH FOR UNITED. MEREDITH WAS THE BEST PLAYER AFIELD, BRINGING HOME A SECOND WINNER'S MEDAL TO ADD TO THE ONE HE WON WITH CITY IN 1904.
WHEN SKIPPER CHARLIE ROBERTS AND HIS VICTORIOUS TEAM RETURNED TO MANCHESTER WITH THE SILVER CUP, THOUSANDS OF HAPPY FANS LINED THE ROUTE.
A YEAR LATER UNITED MOVED AGAIN — TO A THIRD NEW GROUND AT OLD TRAFFORD.
IT WAS TO HOLD 76,962 SPECTATORS FOR AN FA CUP SEMI-FINAL BETWEEN WOLVES AND GRIMSBY IN 1939, MOST OF THEM WERE STANDING — NOT AT ALL LIKE THE THEATRE OF DREAMS WHICH IT IS TODAY!

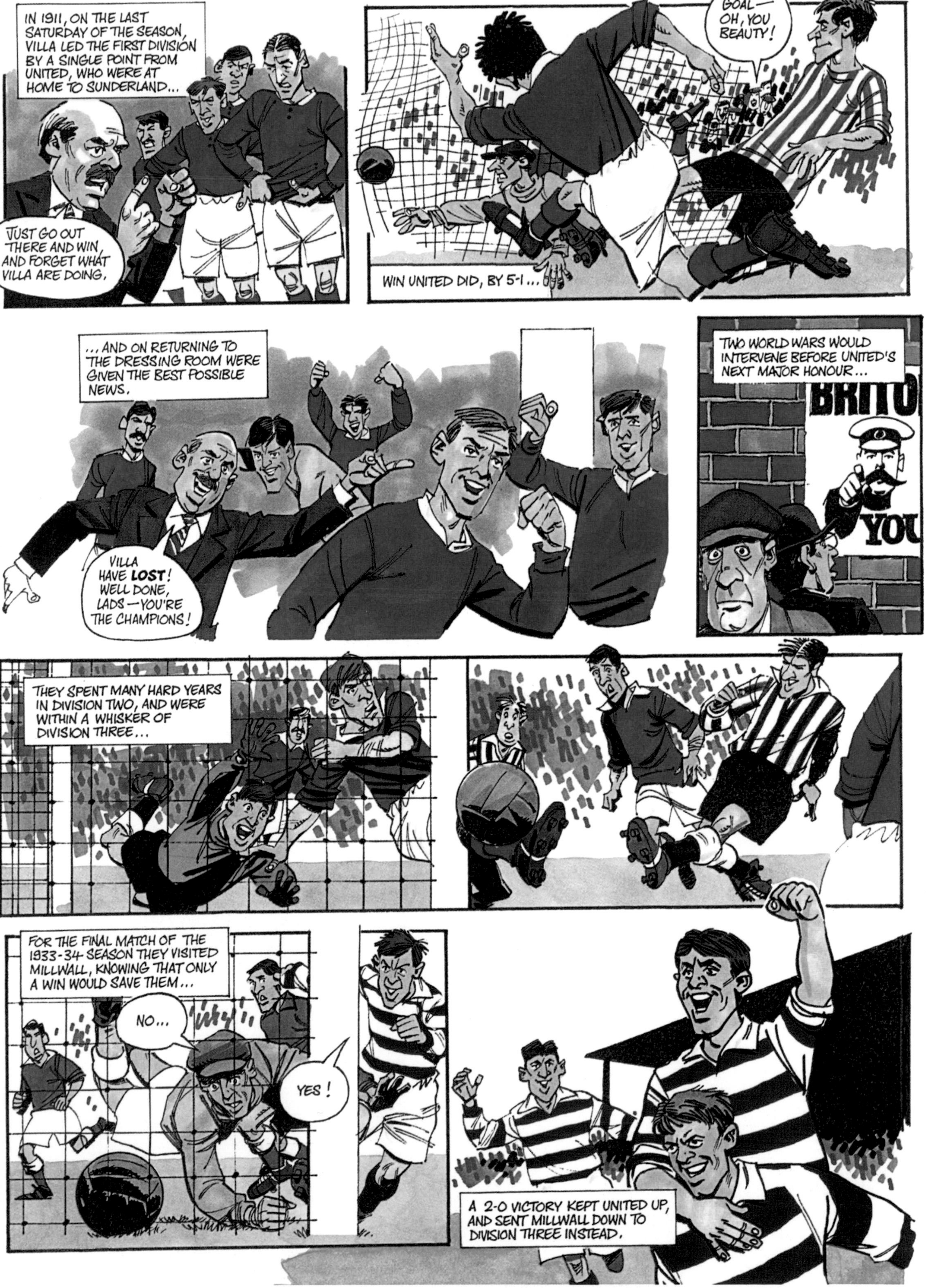
IN 1911, ON THE LAST SATURDAY OF THE SEASON, VILLA LED THE FIRST DIVISION BY A SINGLE POINT FROM UNITED, WHO WERE AT HOME TO SUNDERLAND...
JUST GO OUT THERE AND WIN, AND FORGET WHAT VILLA ARE DOING.
GOAL— OH, YOU BEAUTY!
WIN UNITED DID, BY 5-1...
...AND ON RETURNING TO THE DRESSING ROOM WERE GIVEN THE BEST POSSIBLE NEWS.
VILLA HAVE **LOST**! WELL DONE, LADS—YOU'RE THE CHAMPIONS!
TWO WORLD WARS WOULD INTERVENE BEFORE UNITED'S NEXT MAJOR HONOUR...
BRITO
YOU
THEY SPENT MANY HARD YEARS IN DIVISION TWO, AND WERE WITHIN A WHISKER OF DIVISION THREE...
FOR THE FINAL MATCH OF THE 1933-34 SEASON THEY VISITED MILLWALL, KNOWING THAT ONLY A WIN WOULD SAVE THEM...
NO...
YES!
A 2-0 VICTORY KEPT UNITED UP, AND SENT MILLWALL DOWN TO DIVISION THREE INSTEAD.

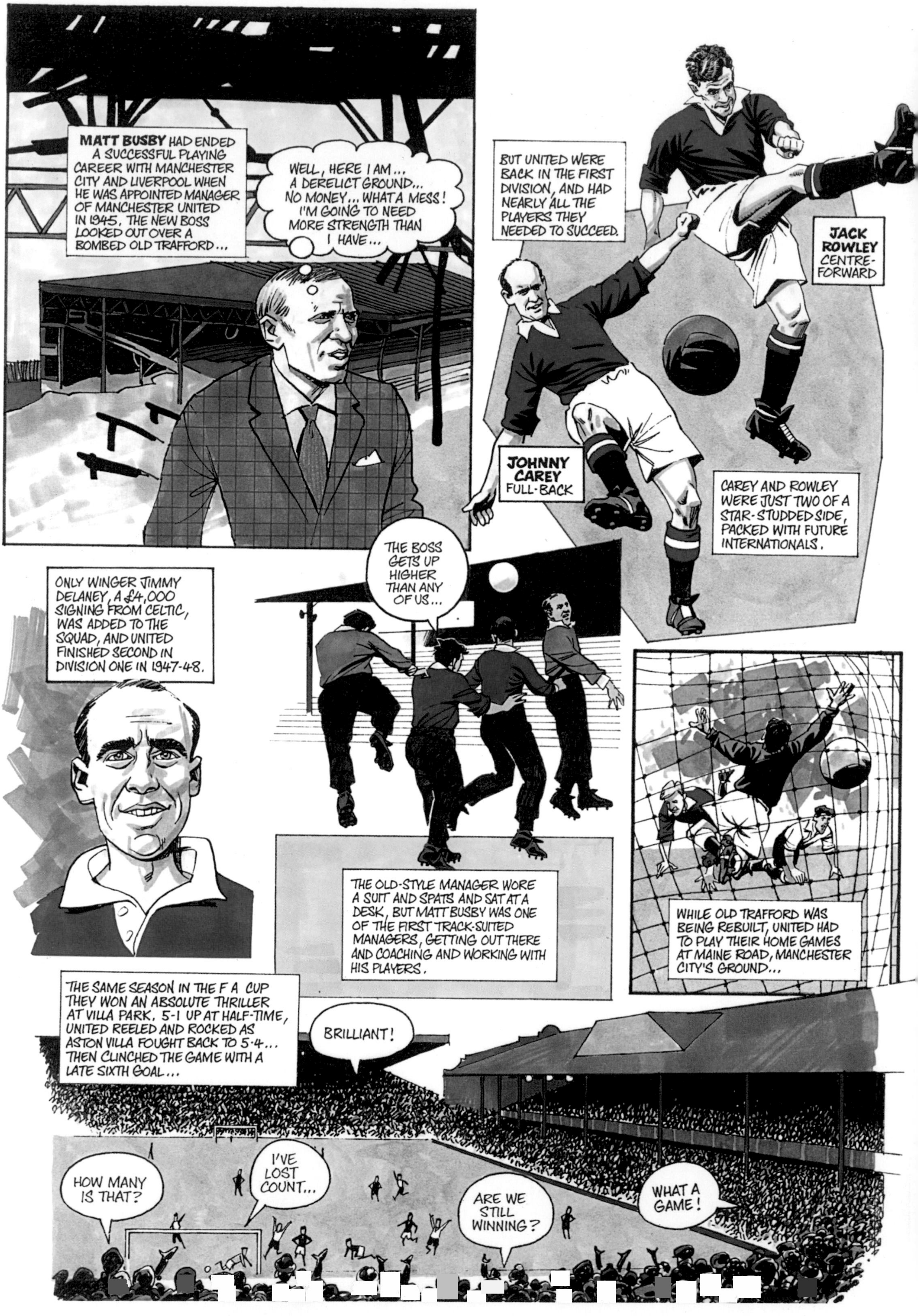

MATT BUSBY HAD ENDED A SUCCESSFUL PLAYING CAREER WITH MANCHESTER CITY AND LIVERPOOL WHEN HE WAS APPOINTED MANAGER OF MANCHESTER UNITED IN 1945. THE NEW BOSS LOOKED OUT OVER A BOMBED OLD TRAFFORD...
WELL, HERE I AM... A DERELICT GROUND... NO MONEY... WHAT A MESS! I'M GOING TO NEED MORE STRENGTH THAN I HAVE...
BUT UNITED WERE BACK IN THE FIRST DIVISION, AND HAD NEARLY ALL THE PLAYERS THEY NEEDED TO SUCCEED.
JACK ROWLEY CENTRE-FORWARD
JOHNNY CAREY FULL-BACK
CAREY AND ROWLEY WERE JUST TWO OF A STAR-STUDDED SIDE, PACKED WITH FUTURE INTERNATIONALS.
ONLY WINGER JIMMY DELANEY, A £4,000 SIGNING FROM CELTIC, WAS ADDED TO THE SQUAD, AND UNITED FINISHED SECOND IN DIVISION ONE IN 1947-48.
THE BOSS GETS UP HIGHER THAN ANY OF US...
THE OLD-STYLE MANAGER WORE A SUIT AND SPATS AND SAT AT A DESK, BUT MATT BUSBY WAS ONE OF THE FIRST TRACK-SUITED MANAGERS, GETTING OUT THERE AND COACHING AND WORKING WITH HIS PLAYERS.
WHILE OLD TRAFFORD WAS BEING REBUILT, UNITED HAD TO PLAY THEIR HOME GAMES AT MAINE ROAD, MANCHESTER CITY'S GROUND...
THE SAME SEASON IN THE F A CUP THEY WON AN ABSOLUTE THRILLER AT VILLA PARK. 5-1 UP AT HALF-TIME, UNITED REELED AND ROCKED AS ASTON VILLA FOUGHT BACK TO 5-4... THEN CLINCHED THE GAME WITH A LATE SIXTH GOAL...
BRILLIANT!
HOW MANY IS THAT?
I'VE LOST COUNT...
ARE WE STILL WINNING?
WHAT A GAME!

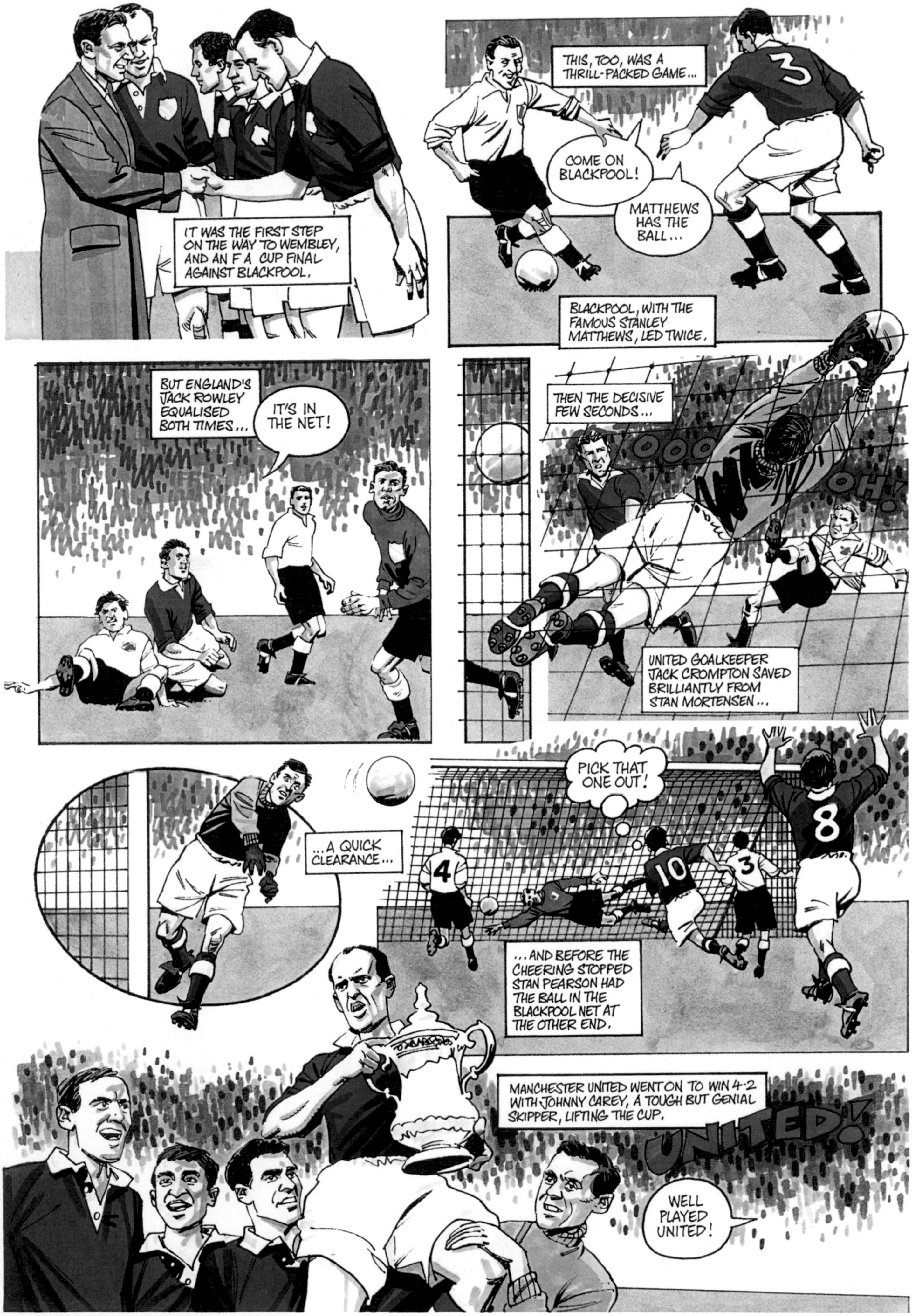
IT WAS THE FIRST STEP ON THE WAY TO WEMBLEY, AND AN F A CUP FINAL AGAINST BLACKPOOL.
THIS, TOO, WAS A THRILL-PACKED GAME...
COME ON BLACKPOOL!
MATTHEWS HAS THE BALL...
BLACKPOOL, WITH THE FAMOUS STANLEY MATTHEWS, LED TWICE.
BUT ENGLAND'S JACK ROWLEY EQUALISED BOTH TIMES...
IT'S IN THE NET!
THEN THE DECISIVE FEW SECONDS...
OOOOH!
UNITED GOALKEEPER JACK CROMPTON SAVED BRILLIANTLY FROM STAN MORTENSEN...
...A QUICK CLEARANCE...
PICK THAT ONE OUT!
...AND BEFORE THE CHEERING STOPPED STAN PEARSON HAD THE BALL IN THE BLACKPOOL NET AT THE OTHER END.
MANCHESTER UNITED WENT ON TO WIN 4-2 WITH JOHNNY CAREY, A TOUGH BUT GENIAL SKIPPER, LIFTING THE CUP.
UNITED!
WELL PLAYED UNITED!

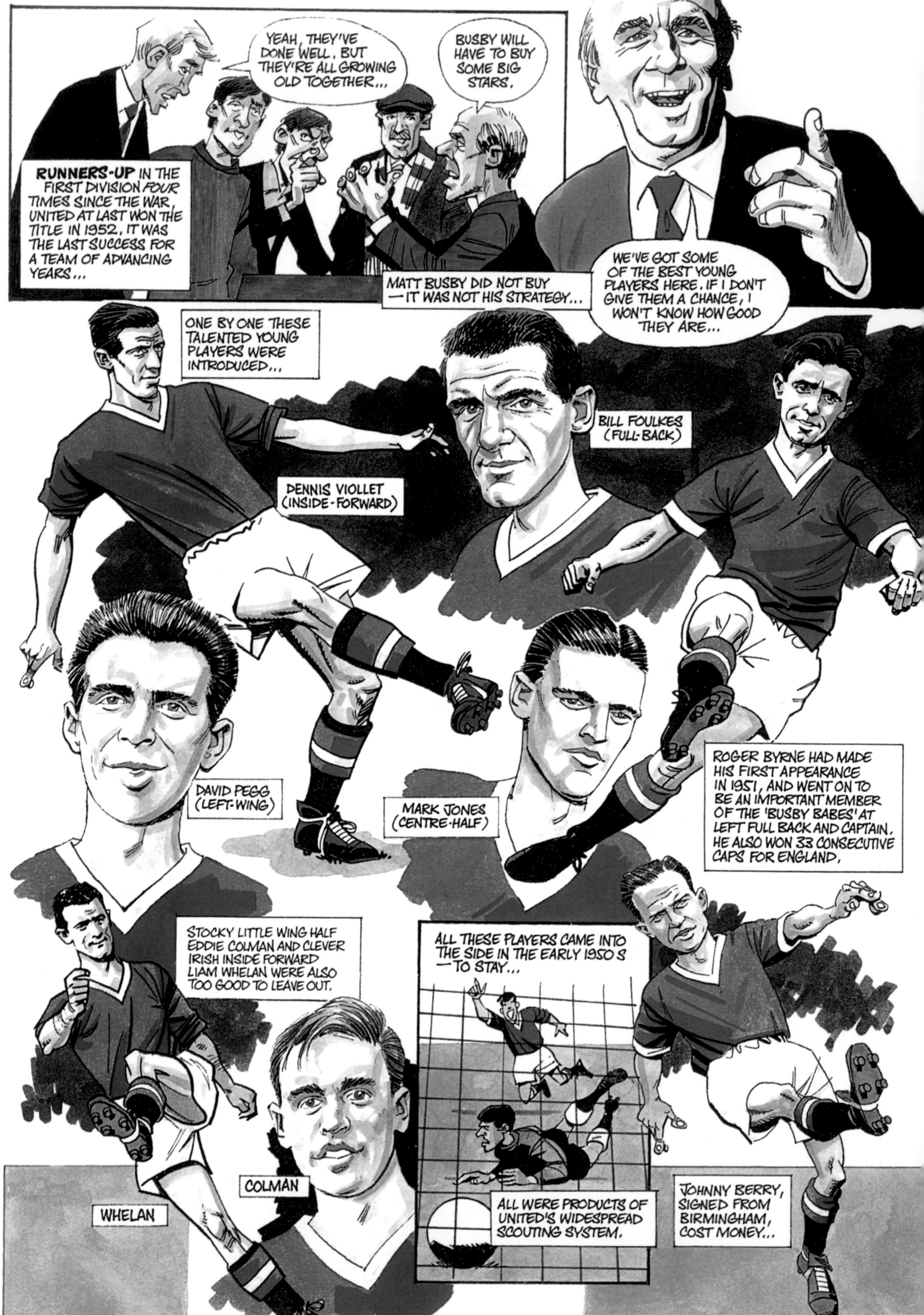

YEAH, THEY'VE DONE WELL. BUT THEY'RE ALL GROWING OLD TOGETHER...
BUSBY WILL HAVE TO BUY SOME BIG STARS.
RUNNERS-UP IN THE FIRST DIVISION FOUR TIMES SINCE THE WAR, UNITED AT LAST WON THE TITLE IN 1952. IT WAS THE LAST SUCCESS FOR A TEAM OF ADVANCING YEARS...
MATT BUSBY DID NOT BUY —IT WAS NOT HIS STRATEGY...
WE'VE GOT SOME OF THE BEST YOUNG PLAYERS HERE. IF I DON'T GIVE THEM A CHANCE, I WON'T KNOW HOW GOOD THEY ARE...
ONE BY ONE THESE TALENTED YOUNG PLAYERS WERE INTRODUCED...
BILL FOULKES (FULL-BACK)
DENNIS VIOLLET (INSIDE-FORWARD)
DAVID PEGG (LEFT-WING)
MARK JONES (CENTRE-HALF)
ROGER BYRNE HAD MADE HIS FIRST APPEARANCE IN 1951, AND WENT ON TO BE AN IMPORTANT MEMBER OF THE 'BUSBY BABES' AT LEFT FULL BACK AND CAPTAIN. HE ALSO WON 33 CONSECUTIVE CAPS FOR ENGLAND.
STOCKY LITTLE WING HALF EDDIE COLMAN AND CLEVER IRISH INSIDE FORWARD LIAM WHELAN WERE ALSO TOO GOOD TO LEAVE OUT.
ALL THESE PLAYERS CAME INTO THE SIDE IN THE EARLY 1950 S —TO STAY...
ALL WERE PRODUCTS OF UNITED'S WIDESPREAD SCOUTING SYSTEM.
WHELAN
COLMAN
JOHNNY BERRY, SIGNED FROM BIRMINGHAM, COST MONEY...

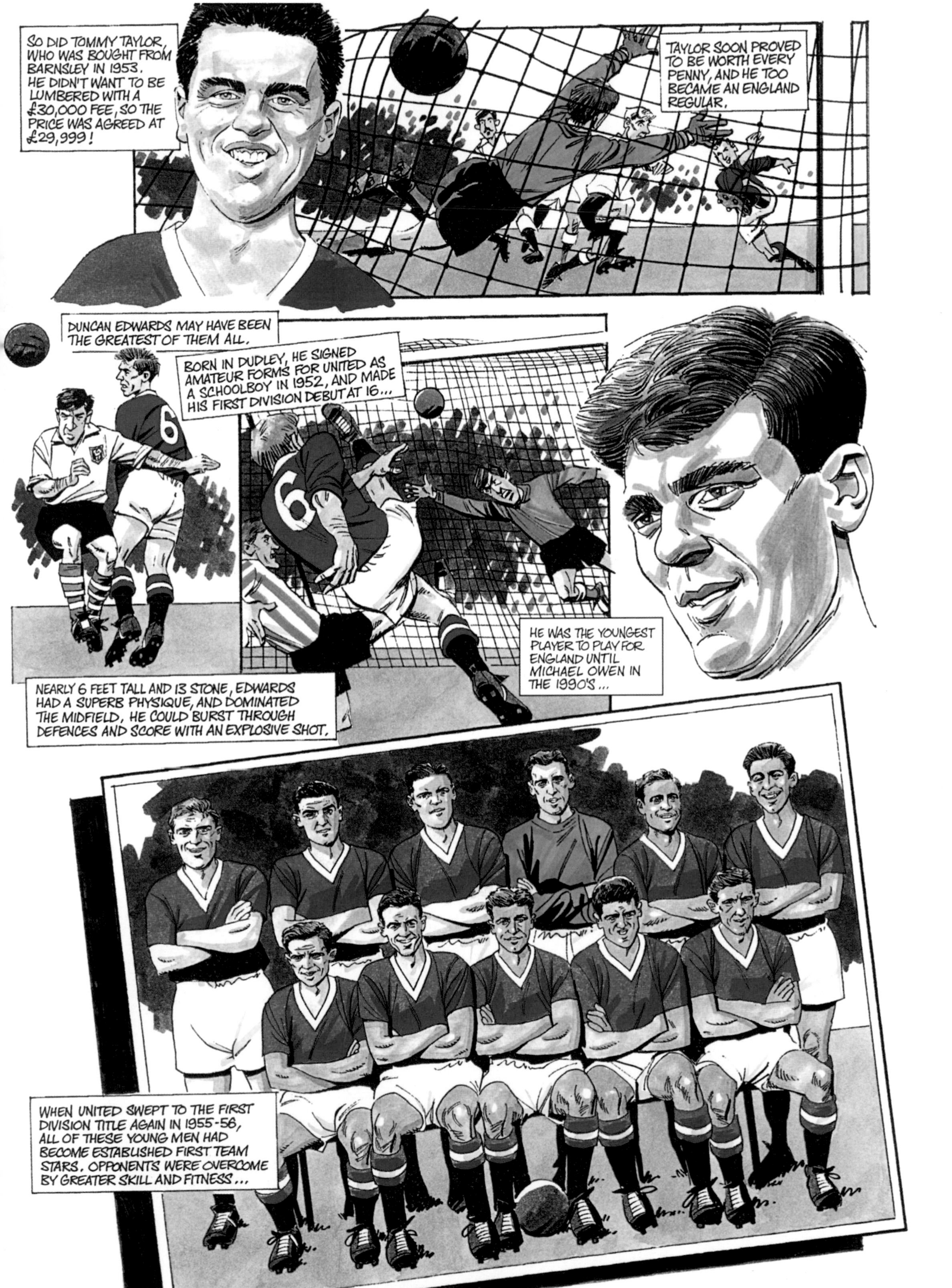
SO DID TOMMY TAYLOR, WHO WAS BOUGHT FROM BARNSLEY IN 1953. HE DIDN'T WANT TO BE LUMBERED WITH A £30,000 FEE, SO THE PRICE WAS AGREED AT £29,999!
TAYLOR SOON PROVED TO BE WORTH EVERY PENNY, AND HE TOO BECAME AN ENGLAND REGULAR.
DUNCAN EDWARDS MAY HAVE BEEN THE GREATEST OF THEM ALL.
BORN IN DUDLEY, HE SIGNED AMATEUR FORMS FOR UNITED AS A SCHOOLBOY IN 1952, AND MADE HIS FIRST DIVISION DEBUT AT 16...
HE WAS THE YOUNGEST PLAYER TO PLAY FOR ENGLAND UNTIL MICHAEL OWEN IN THE 1990'S...
NEARLY 6 FEET TALL AND 13 STONE, EDWARDS HAD A SUPERB PHYSIQUE, AND DOMINATED THE MIDFIELD, HE COULD BURST THROUGH DEFENCES AND SCORE WITH AN EXPLOSIVE SHOT.
WHEN UNITED SWEPT TO THE FIRST DIVISION TITLE AGAIN IN 1955-56, ALL OF THESE YOUNG MEN HAD BECOME ESTABLISHED FIRST TEAM STARS. OPPONENTS WERE OVERCOME BY GREATER SKILL AND FITNESS...

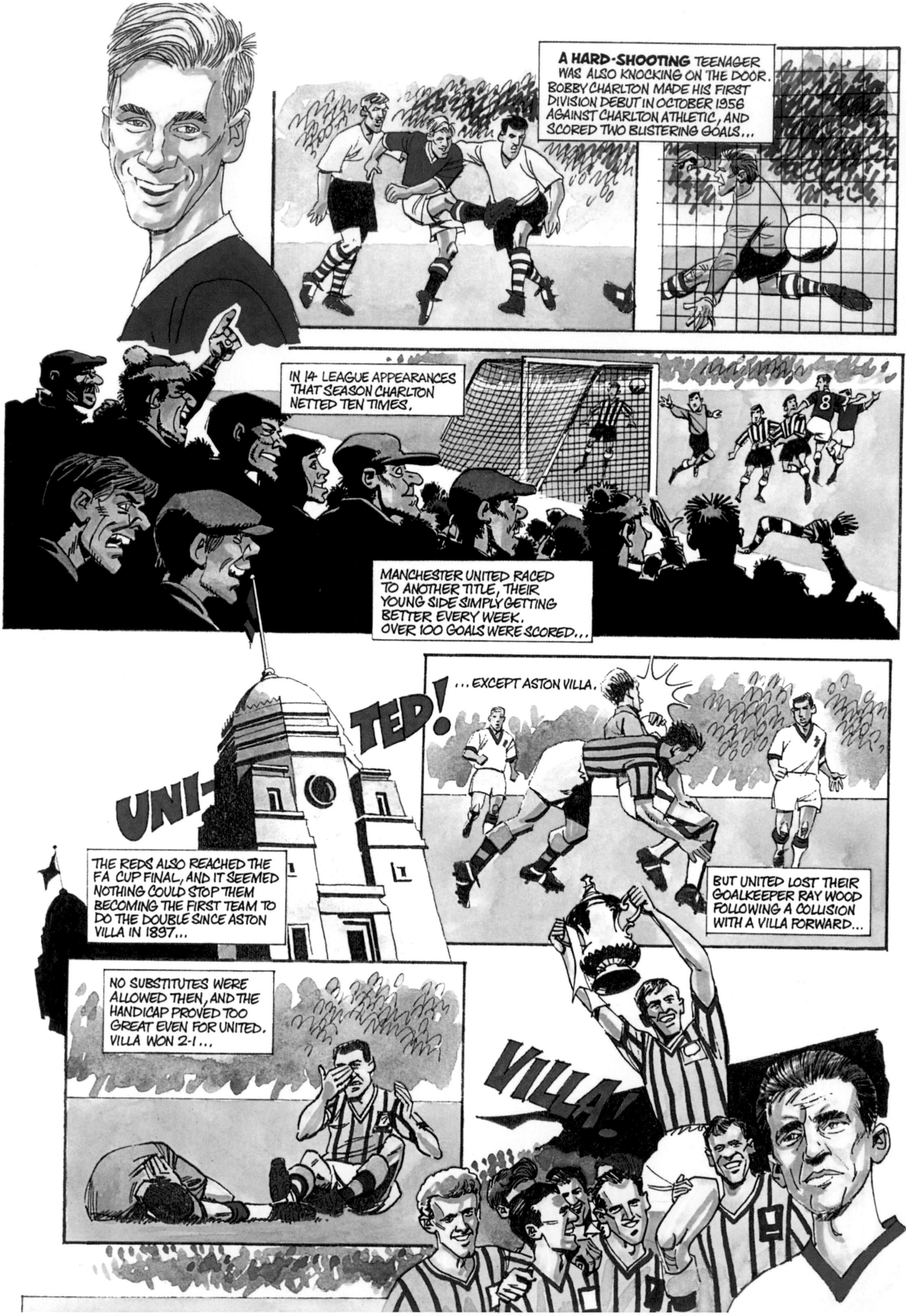

A HARD-SHOOTING TEENAGER WAS ALSO KNOCKING ON THE DOOR. BOBBY CHARLTON MADE HIS FIRST DIVISION DEBUT IN OCTOBER 1956 AGAINST CHARLTON ATHLETIC, AND SCORED TWO BLISTERING GOALS...
IN 14 LEAGUE APPEARANCES THAT SEASON CHARLTON NETTED TEN TIMES.
MANCHESTER UNITED RACED TO ANOTHER TITLE, THEIR YOUNG SIDE SIMPLY GETTING BETTER EVERY WEEK. OVER 100 GOALS WERE SCORED...
UNI-
TED!
THE REDS ALSO REACHED THE FA CUP FINAL, AND IT SEEMED NOTHING COULD STOP THEM BECOMING THE FIRST TEAM TO DO THE DOUBLE SINCE ASTON VILLA IN 1897...
...EXCEPT ASTON VILLA.
BUT UNITED LOST THEIR GOALKEEPER RAY WOOD FOLLOWING A COLLISION WITH A VILLA FORWARD...
NO SUBSTITUTES WERE ALLOWED THEN, AND THE HANDICAP PROVED TOO GREAT EVEN FOR UNITED. VILLA WON 2-1...
VILLA!

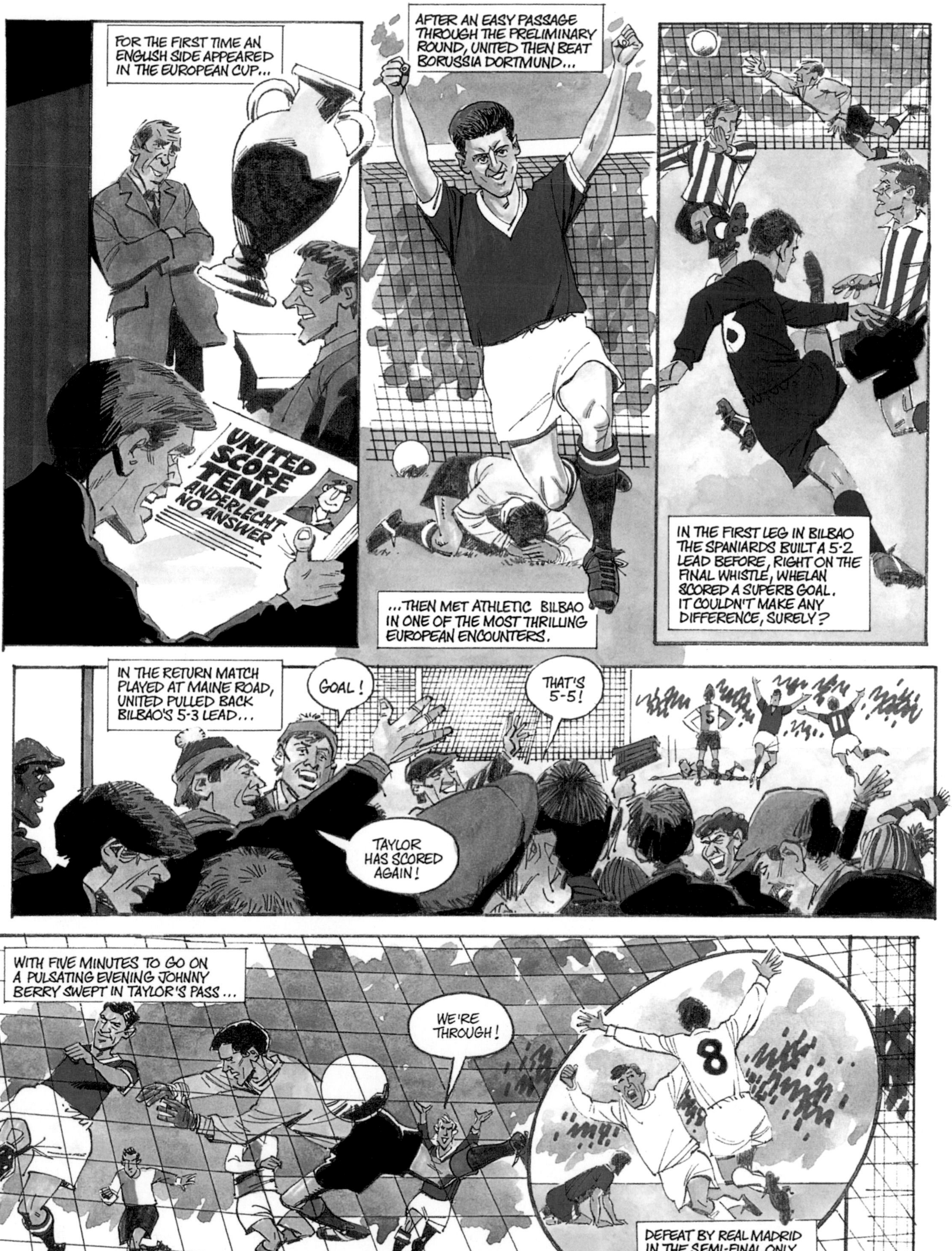
FOR THE FIRST TIME AN ENGLISH SIDE APPEARED IN THE EUROPEAN CUP...
UNITED SCORE TEN! ANDERLECHT NO ANSWER
AFTER AN EASY PASSAGE THROUGH THE PRELIMINARY ROUND, UNITED THEN BEAT BORUSSIA DORTMUND...
...THEN MET ATHLETIC BILBAO IN ONE OF THE MOST THRILLING EUROPEAN ENCOUNTERS.
IN THE FIRST LEG IN BILBAO THE SPANIARDS BUILT A 5-2 LEAD BEFORE, RIGHT ON THE FINAL WHISTLE, WHELAN SCORED A SUPERB GOAL. IT COULDN'T MAKE ANY DIFFERENCE, SURELY?
IN THE RETURN MATCH PLAYED AT MAINE ROAD, UNITED PULLED BACK BILBAO'S 5-3 LEAD...
GOAL!
TAYLOR HAS SCORED AGAIN!
THAT'S 5-5!
WITH FIVE MINUTES TO GO ON A PULSATING EVENING JOHNNY BERRY SWEPT IN TAYLOR'S PASS...
WE'RE THROUGH!
DEFEAT BY REAL MADRID IN THE SEMI-FINAL ONLY SERVED TO STRENGTHEN MATT BUSBY'S RESOLVE TO SUCCEED IN EUROPE...

IN FEBRUARY 1958, RETURNING FROM A SUCCESSFUL EUROPEAN CUP MATCH AGAINST RED STAR BELGRADE, THE PLANE CARRYING UNITED'S BRILLIANT YOUNG TEAM CRASHED AT MUNICH AIRPORT. MARK JONES, TOMMY TAYLOR, ROGER BYRNE, GEOFF BENT, EDDIE COLMAN, LIAM WHELAN AND DAVID PEGG WERE KILLED, AND DUNCAN EDWARDS DIED LATER FROM HIS INJURIES. IN ALL 23 PEOPLE DIED IN THE CRASH BUT SOME PLAYERS SURVIVED, AS WELL AS THEIR MANAGER MATT BUSBY, WHO BRAVELY REPEATED HIS DESIRE TO CONQUER EUROPE.

TWO WEEKS AFTER THE DISASTER MANCHESTER UNITED, PATCHED UP WITH RESERVES AND NEW SIGNINGS, BEAT SHEFFIELD WEDNESDAY 3-0 IN FRONT OF 60,000 TEARFUL FANS.

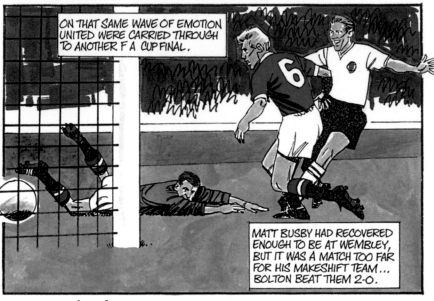

ON THAT SAME WAVE OF EMOTION UNITED WERE CARRIED THROUGH TO ANOTHER F A CUP FINAL.

MATT BUSBY HAD RECOVERED ENOUGH TO BE AT WEMBLEY, BUT IT WAS A MATCH TOO FAR FOR HIS MAKESHIFT TEAM ... BOLTON BEAT THEM 2-0.

IT WAS TO BE FIVE YEARS BEFORE UNITED REACHED WEMBLEY AGAIN ...

BUSBY EMPTIED THE COFFERS TO BUY DENIS LAW FROM TORINO IN 1962, AND LAW SCORED THE FIRST GOAL IN THE FINAL OF 1963 AGAINST LEICESTER CITY.

UNITED HAD STRUGGLED IN THE LEAGUE BUT WON THE CUP 3-1. BILL FOULKES AND BOBBY CHARLTON WERE TWO OF THE SURVIVORS OF MUNICH, AND AFTER BEING LOSERS IN 1957 AND 1958, BOTH GAINED WINNERS' MEDALS AT LAST.

LAW WAS A SUPERB GOALSCORER, HE COULD SNIFF THE MEREST HALF-CHANCE. WHERE THAT CHANCE FELL, LAW WOULD BE THERE. IN 1963-64 HE SCORED 46 LEAGUE AND CUP GOALS IN 41 GAMES, INCLUDING SEVEN HAT-TRICKS.

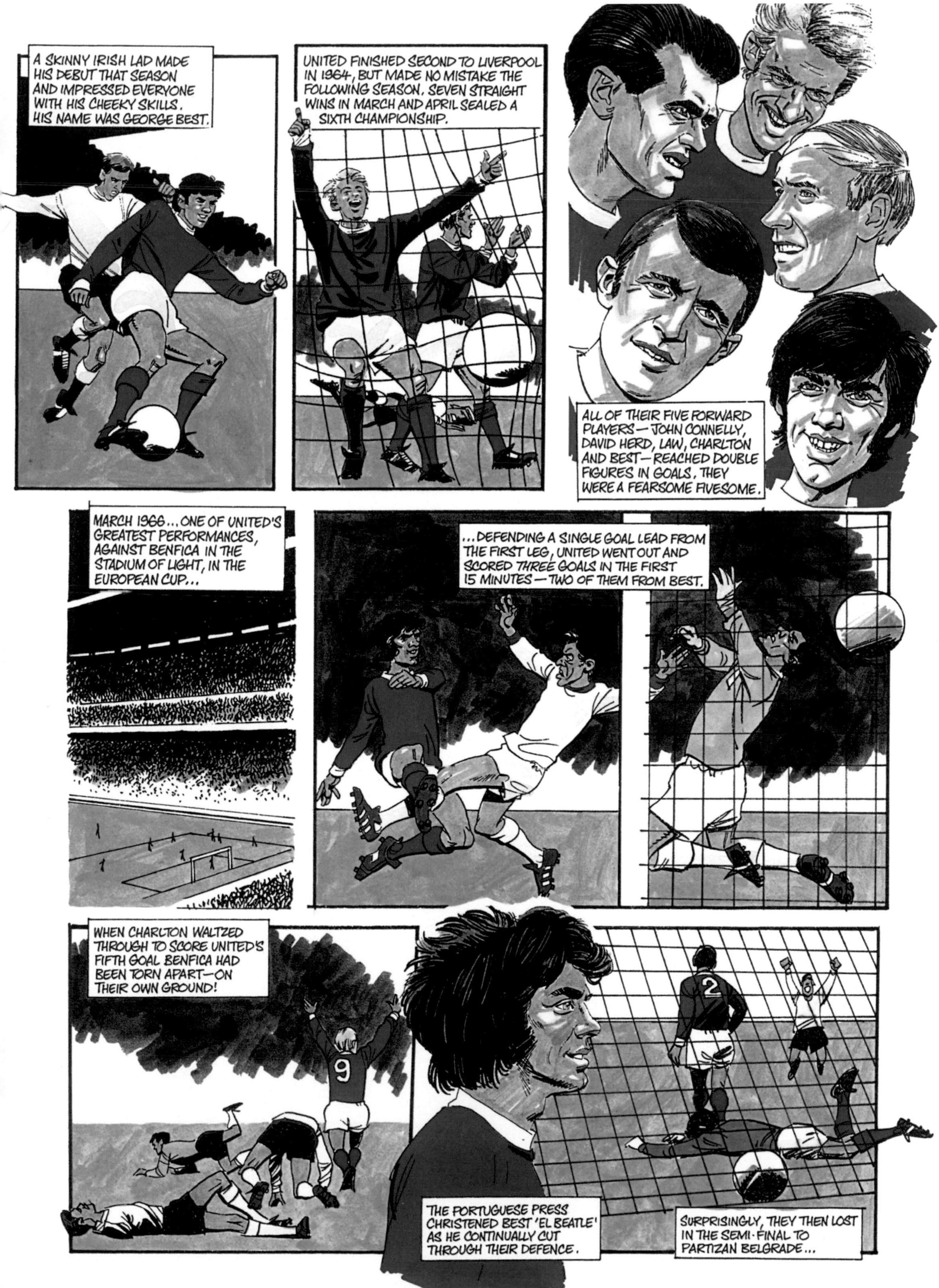
A SKINNY IRISH LAD MADE HIS DEBUT THAT SEASON AND IMPRESSED EVERYONE WITH HIS CHEEKY SKILLS. HIS NAME WAS GEORGE BEST.
UNITED FINISHED SECOND TO LIVERPOOL IN 1964, BUT MADE NO MISTAKE THE FOLLOWING SEASON. SEVEN STRAIGHT WINS IN MARCH AND APRIL SEALED A SIXTH CHAMPIONSHIP.
ALL OF THEIR FIVE FORWARD PLAYERS — JOHN CONNELLY, DAVID HERD, LAW, CHARLTON AND BEST — REACHED DOUBLE FIGURES IN GOALS. THEY WERE A FEARSOME FIVESOME.
MARCH 1966... ONE OF UNITED'S GREATEST PERFORMANCES, AGAINST BENFICA IN THE STADIUM OF LIGHT, IN THE EUROPEAN CUP...
...DEFENDING A SINGLE GOAL LEAD FROM THE FIRST LEG, UNITED WENT OUT AND SCORED THREE GOALS IN THE FIRST 15 MINUTES — TWO OF THEM FROM BEST.
WHEN CHARLTON WALTZED THROUGH TO SCORE UNITED'S FIFTH GOAL BENFICA HAD BEEN TORN APART — ON THEIR OWN GROUND!
9
2
THE PORTUGUESE PRESS CHRISTENED BEST 'EL BEATLE' AS HE CONTINUALLY CUT THROUGH THEIR DEFENCE.
SURPRISINGLY, THEY THEN LOST IN THE SEMI-FINAL TO PARTIZAN BELGRADE...

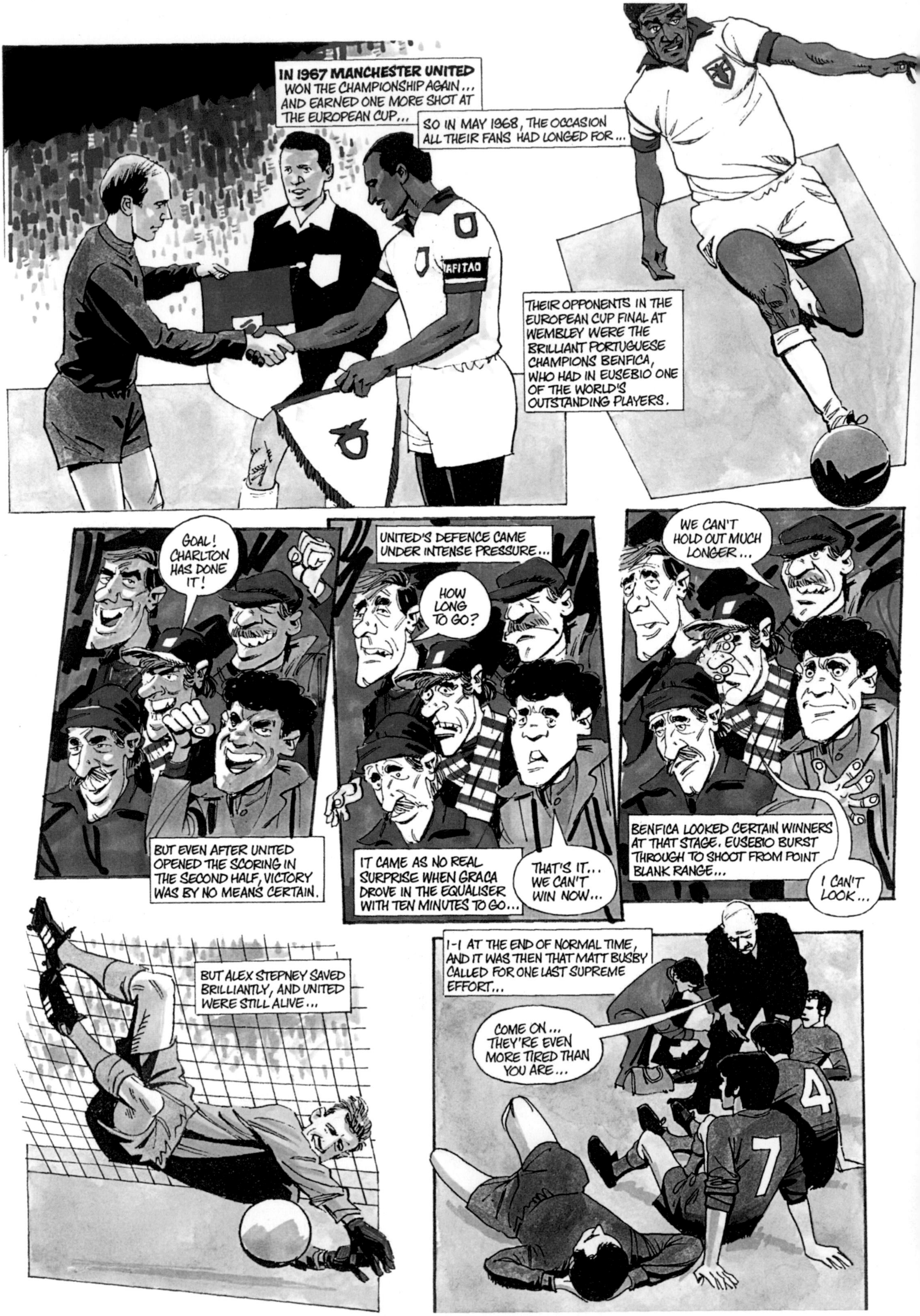
IN 1967 MANCHESTER UNITED WON THE CHAMPIONSHIP AGAIN... AND EARNED ONE MORE SHOT AT THE EUROPEAN CUP...
SO IN MAY 1968, THE OCCASION ALL THEIR FANS HAD LONGED FOR...
THEIR OPPONENTS IN THE EUROPEAN CUP FINAL AT WEMBLEY WERE THE BRILLIANT PORTUGUESE CHAMPIONS BENFICA, WHO HAD IN EUSEBIO ONE OF THE WORLD'S OUTSTANDING PLAYERS.
GOAL! CHARLTON HAS DONE IT!
BUT EVEN AFTER UNITED OPENED THE SCORING IN THE SECOND HALF, VICTORY WAS BY NO MEANS CERTAIN.
UNITED'S DEFENCE CAME UNDER INTENSE PRESSURE...
HOW LONG TO GO?
IT CAME AS NO REAL SURPRISE WHEN GRACA DROVE IN THE EQUALISER WITH TEN MINUTES TO GO...
THAT'S IT... WE CAN'T WIN NOW...
WE CAN'T HOLD OUT MUCH LONGER...
BENFICA LOOKED CERTAIN WINNERS AT THAT STAGE. EUSEBIO BURST THROUGH TO SHOOT FROM POINT BLANK RANGE...
I CAN'T LOOK...
BUT ALEX STEPNEY SAVED BRILLIANTLY, AND UNITED WERE STILL ALIVE...
1-1 AT THE END OF NORMAL TIME, AND IT WAS THEN THAT MATT BUSBY CALLED FOR ONE LAST SUPREME EFFORT...
COME ON... THEY'RE EVEN MORE TIRED THAN YOU ARE...

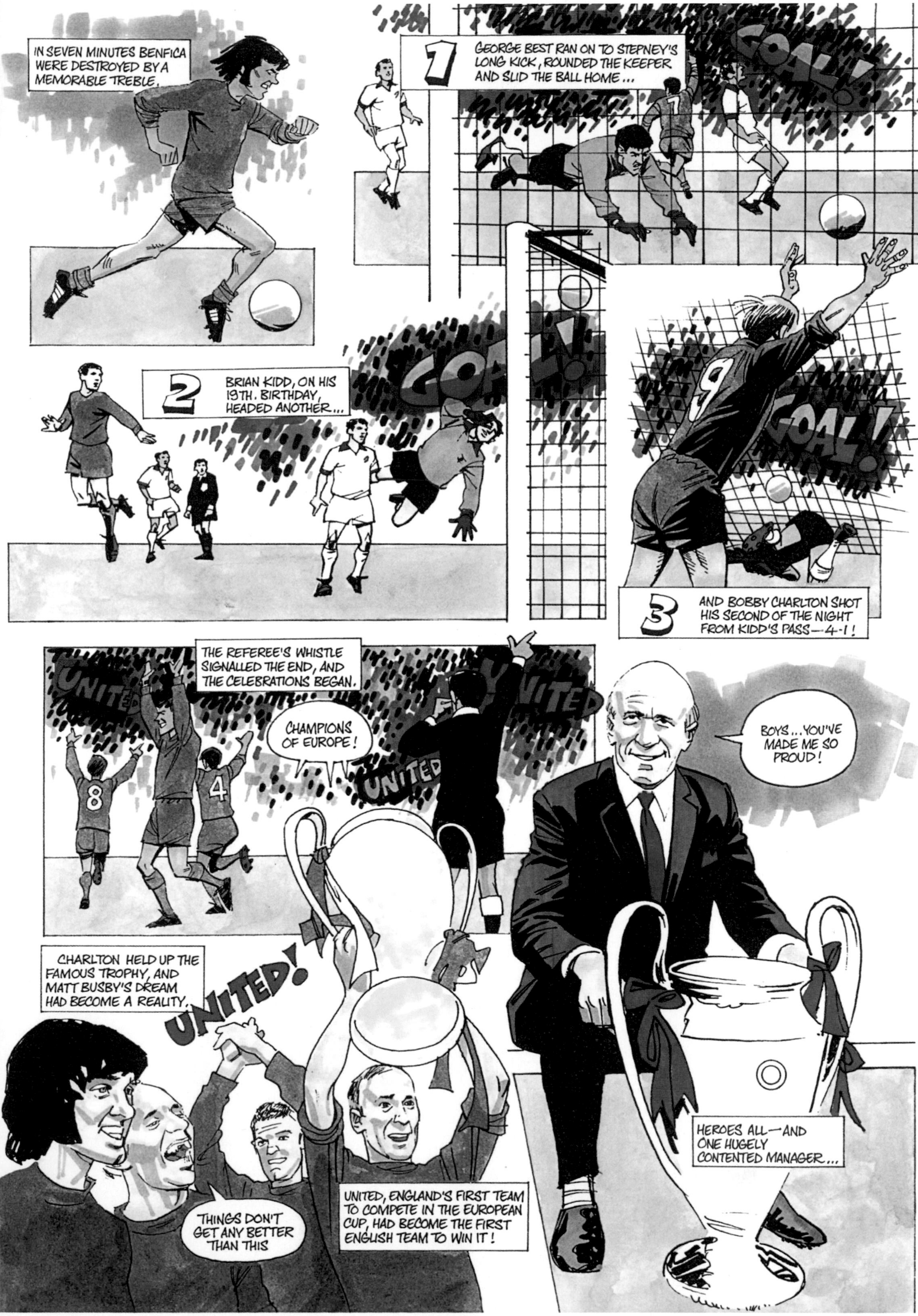
IN SEVEN MINUTES BENFICA WERE DESTROYED BY A MEMORABLE TREBLE.
1
GEORGE BEST RAN ON TO STEPNEY'S LONG KICK, ROUNDED THE KEEPER AND SLID THE BALL HOME ...
GOAL!
2
BRIAN KIDD, ON HIS 19TH. BIRTHDAY, HEADED ANOTHER...
GOAL!
GOAL!
3
AND BOBBY CHARLTON SHOT HIS SECOND OF THE NIGHT FROM KIDD'S PASS—4-1!
THE REFEREE'S WHISTLE SIGNALLED THE END, AND THE CELEBRATIONS BEGAN.
UNITED
UNITED
CHAMPIONS OF EUROPE!
UNITED
BOYS... YOU'VE MADE ME SO PROUD!
CHARLTON HELD UP THE FAMOUS TROPHY, AND MATT BUSBY'S DREAM HAD BECOME A REALITY.
UNITED!
HEROES ALL—AND ONE HUGELY CONTENTED MANAGER...
THINGS DON'T GET ANY BETTER THAN THIS
UNITED, ENGLAND'S FIRST TEAM TO COMPETE IN THE EUROPEAN CUP, HAD BECOME THE FIRST ENGLISH TEAM TO WIN IT!

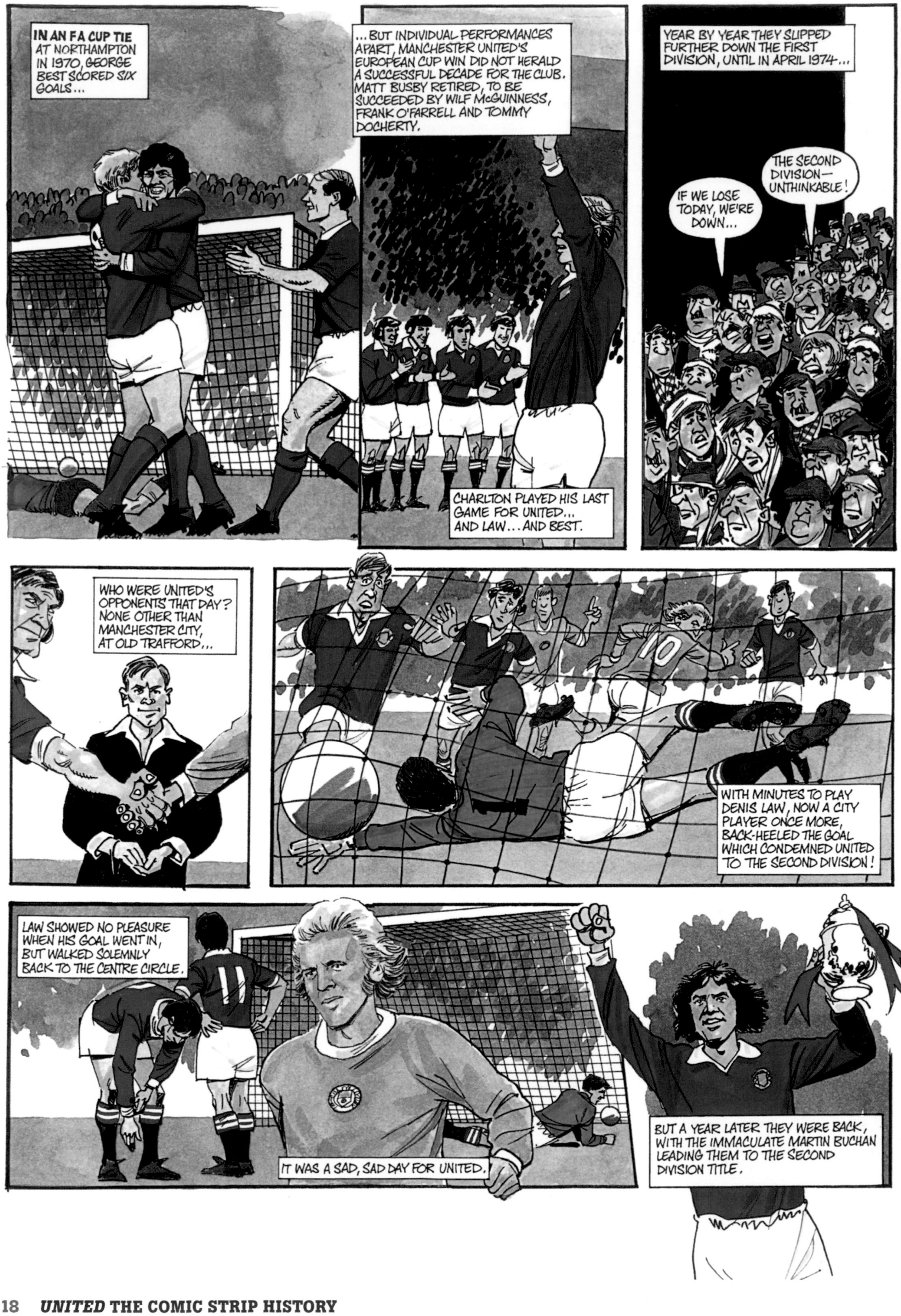
IN AN FA CUP TIE AT NORTHAMPTON IN 1970, GEORGE BEST SCORED SIX GOALS...
...BUT INDIVIDUAL PERFORMANCES APART, MANCHESTER UNITED'S EUROPEAN CUP WIN DID NOT HERALD A SUCCESSFUL DECADE FOR THE CLUB. MATT BUSBY RETIRED, TO BE SUCCEEDED BY WILF McGUINNESS, FRANK O'FARRELL AND TOMMY DOCHERTY.
CHARLTON PLAYED HIS LAST GAME FOR UNITED... AND LAW... AND BEST.
YEAR BY YEAR THEY SLIPPED FURTHER DOWN THE FIRST DIVISION, UNTIL IN APRIL 1974...
IF WE LOSE TODAY, WE'RE DOWN...
THE SECOND DIVISION— UNTHINKABLE!
WHO WERE UNITED'S OPPONENTS THAT DAY? NONE OTHER THAN MANCHESTER CITY, AT OLD TRAFFORD...
WITH MINUTES TO PLAY DENIS LAW, NOW A CITY PLAYER ONCE MORE, BACK-HEELED THE GOAL WHICH CONDEMNED UNITED TO THE SECOND DIVISION!
LAW SHOWED NO PLEASURE WHEN HIS GOAL WENT IN, BUT WALKED SOLEMNLY BACK TO THE CENTRE CIRCLE.
IT WAS A SAD, SAD DAY FOR UNITED.
BUT A YEAR LATER THEY WERE BACK, WITH THE IMMACULATE MARTIN BUCHAN LEADING THEM TO THE SECOND DIVISION TITLE.

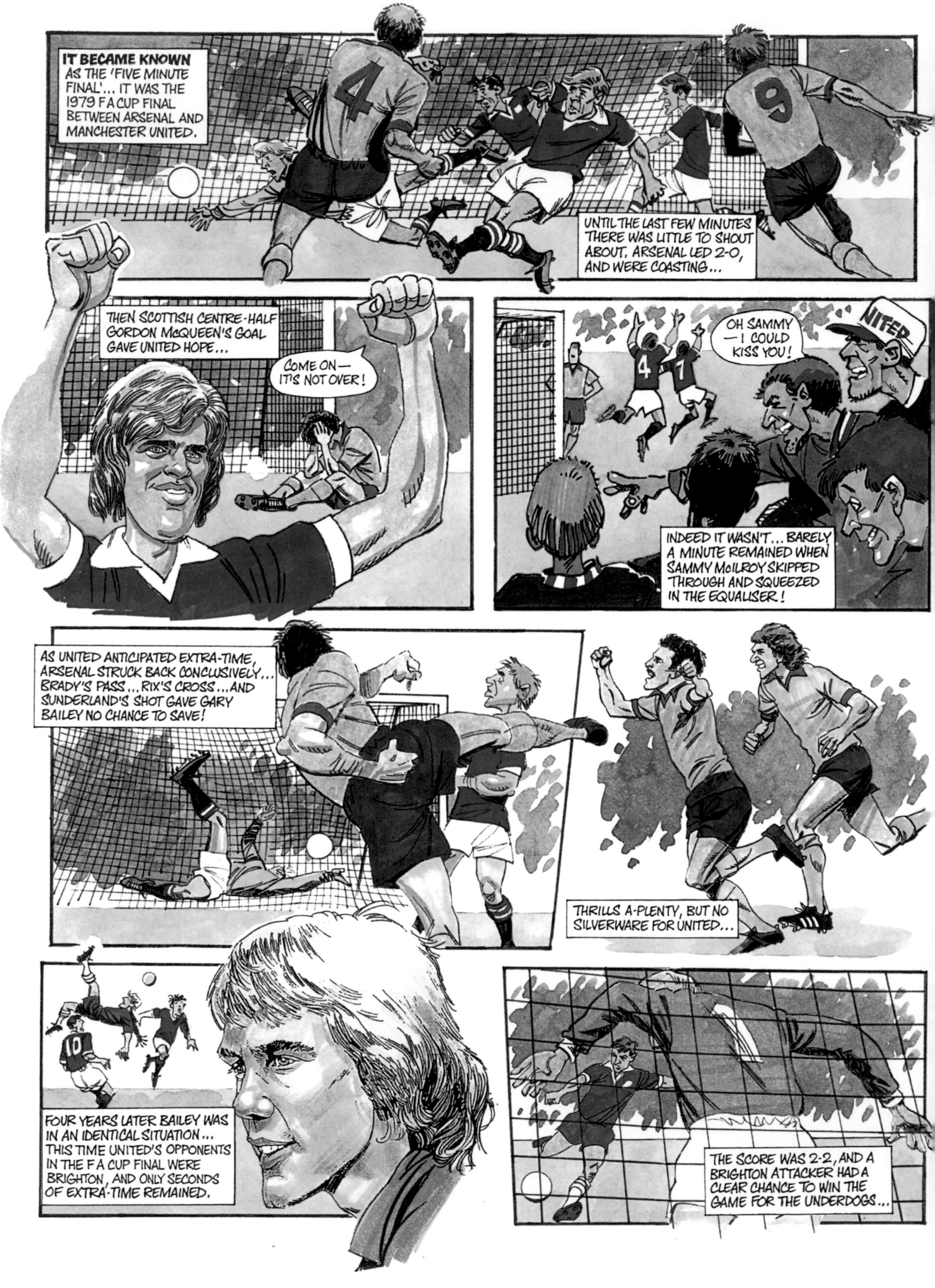
IT BECAME KNOWN AS THE 'FIVE MINUTE FINAL'... IT WAS THE 1979 F A CUP FINAL BETWEEN ARSENAL AND MANCHESTER UNITED.
UNTIL THE LAST FEW MINUTES THERE WAS LITTLE TO SHOUT ABOUT. ARSENAL LED 2-0, AND WERE COASTING...
THEN SCOTTISH CENTRE-HALF GORDON McQUEEN'S GOAL GAVE UNITED HOPE...
COME ON— IT'S NOT OVER!
OH SAMMY —I COULD KISS YOU!
INDEED IT WASN'T... BARELY A MINUTE REMAINED WHEN SAMMY McILROY SKIPPED THROUGH AND SQUEEZED IN THE EQUALISER!
AS UNITED ANTICIPATED EXTRA-TIME, ARSENAL STRUCK BACK CONCLUSIVELY... BRADY'S PASS... RIX'S CROSS... AND SUNDERLAND'S SHOT GAVE GARY BAILEY NO CHANCE TO SAVE!
THRILLS A-PLENTY, BUT NO SILVERWARE FOR UNITED...
FOUR YEARS LATER BAILEY WAS IN AN IDENTICAL SITUATION... THIS TIME UNITED'S OPPONENTS IN THE F A CUP FINAL WERE BRIGHTON, AND ONLY SECONDS OF EXTRA-TIME REMAINED.
THE SCORE WAS 2-2, AND A BRIGHTON ATTACKER HAD A CLEAR CHANCE TO WIN THE GAME FOR THE UNDERDOGS...

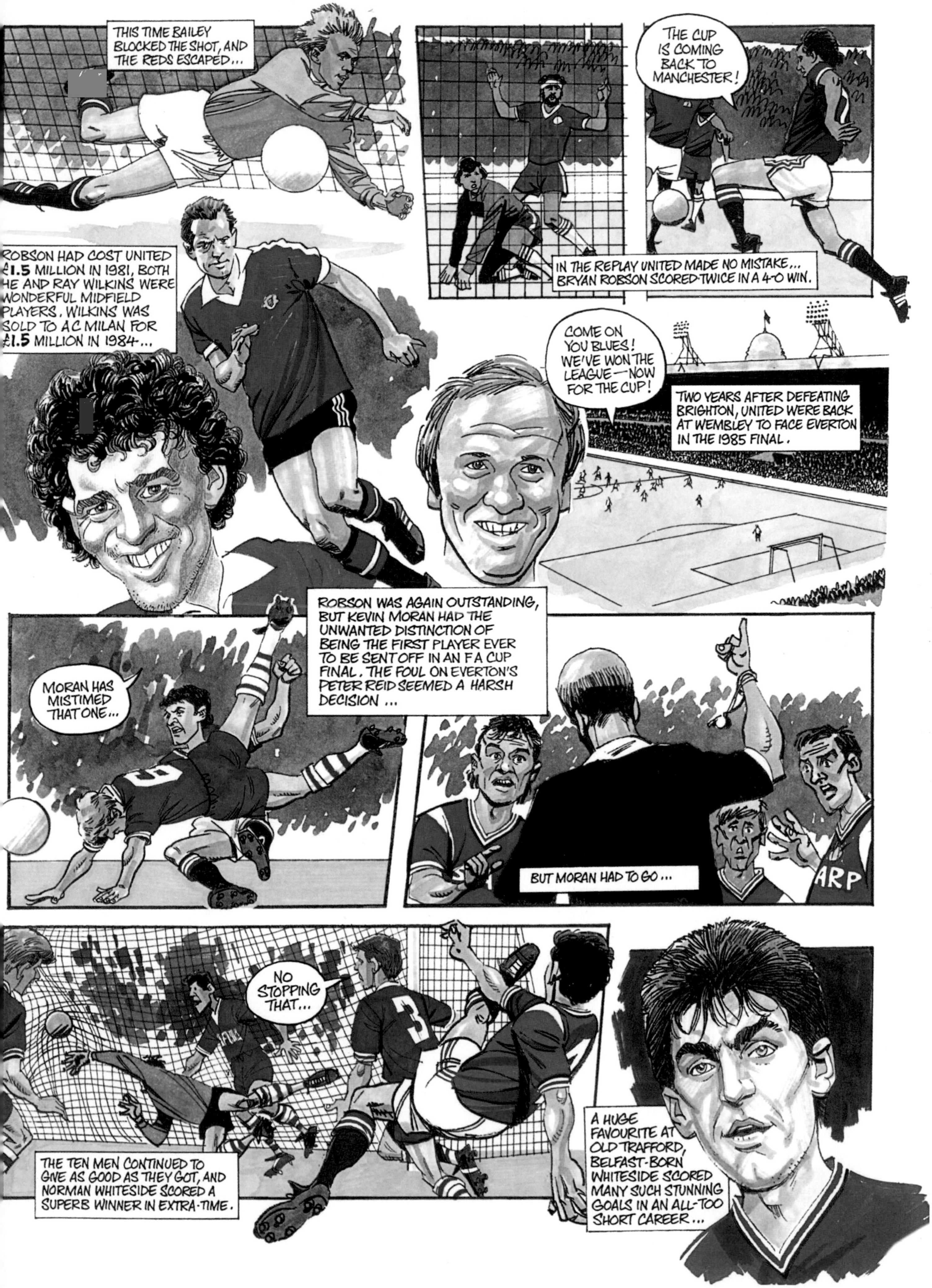

THIS TIME BAILEY BLOCKED THE SHOT, AND THE REDS ESCAPED...
IN THE REPLAY UNITED MADE NO MISTAKE... BRYAN ROBSON SCORED TWICE IN A 4-0 WIN.
THE CUP IS COMING BACK TO MANCHESTER!
ROBSON HAD COST UNITED £1.5 MILLION IN 1981, BOTH HE AND RAY WILKINS WERE WONDERFUL MIDFIELD PLAYERS. WILKINS WAS SOLD TO AC MILAN FOR £1.5 MILLION IN 1984...
COME ON YOU BLUES! WE'VE WON THE LEAGUE—NOW FOR THE CUP!
TWO YEARS AFTER DEFEATING BRIGHTON, UNITED WERE BACK AT WEMBLEY TO FACE EVERTON IN THE 1985 FINAL.
ROBSON WAS AGAIN OUTSTANDING, BUT KEVIN MORAN HAD THE UNWANTED DISTINCTION OF BEING THE FIRST PLAYER EVER TO BE SENT OFF IN AN FA CUP FINAL. THE FOUL ON EVERTON'S PETER REID SEEMED A HARSH DECISION ...
MORAN HAS MISTIMED THAT ONE...
BUT MORAN HAD TO GO...
NO STOPPING THAT...
THE TEN MEN CONTINUED TO GIVE AS GOOD AS THEY GOT, AND NORMAN WHITESIDE SCORED A SUPERB WINNER IN EXTRA-TIME.
A HUGE FAVOURITE AT OLD TRAFFORD, BELFAST-BORN WHITESIDE SCORED MANY SUCH STUNNING GOALS IN AN ALL-TOO SHORT CAREER...

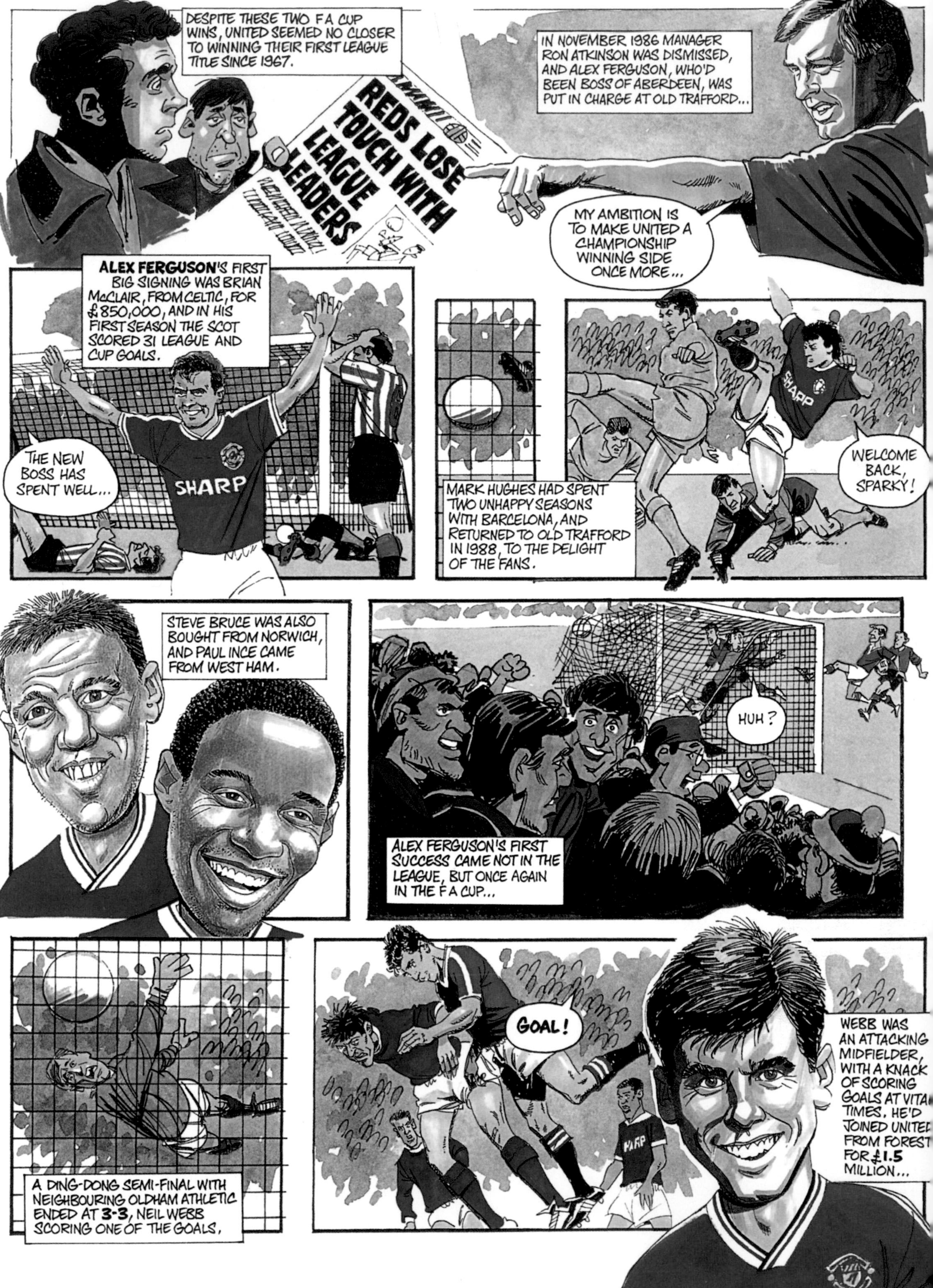
DESPITE THESE TWO F A CUP WINS, UNITED SEEMED NO CLOSER TO WINNING THEIR FIRST LEAGUE TITLE SINCE 1967.
REDS LOSE TOUCH WITH LEAGUE LEADERS
IN NOVEMBER 1986 MANAGER RON ATKINSON WAS DISMISSED, AND ALEX FERGUSON, WHO'D BEEN BOSS OF ABERDEEN, WAS PUT IN CHARGE AT OLD TRAFFORD...
MY AMBITION IS TO MAKE UNITED A CHAMPIONSHIP WINNING SIDE ONCE MORE...
ALEX FERGUSON'S FIRST BIG SIGNING WAS BRIAN McCLAIR, FROM CELTIC, FOR £850,000, AND IN HIS FIRST SEASON THE SCOT SCORED 31 LEAGUE AND CUP GOALS.
THE NEW BOSS HAS SPENT WELL...
SHARP
SHARP
MARK HUGHES HAD SPENT TWO UNHAPPY SEASONS WITH BARCELONA, AND RETURNED TO OLD TRAFFORD IN 1988, TO THE DELIGHT OF THE FANS.
WELCOME BACK, SPARKY!
STEVE BRUCE WAS ALSO BOUGHT FROM NORWICH, AND PAUL INCE CAME FROM WEST HAM.
HUH?
ALEX FERGUSON'S FIRST SUCCESS CAME NOT IN THE LEAGUE, BUT ONCE AGAIN IN THE F A CUP...
A DING-DONG SEMI-FINAL WITH NEIGHBOURING OLDHAM ATHLETIC ENDED AT 3-3, NEIL WEBB SCORING ONE OF THE GOALS,
GOAL!
WEBB WAS AN ATTACKING MIDFIELDER, WITH A KNACK OF SCORING GOALS AT VITA TIMES. HE'D JOINED UNITE FROM FOREST FOR £1.5 MILLION...

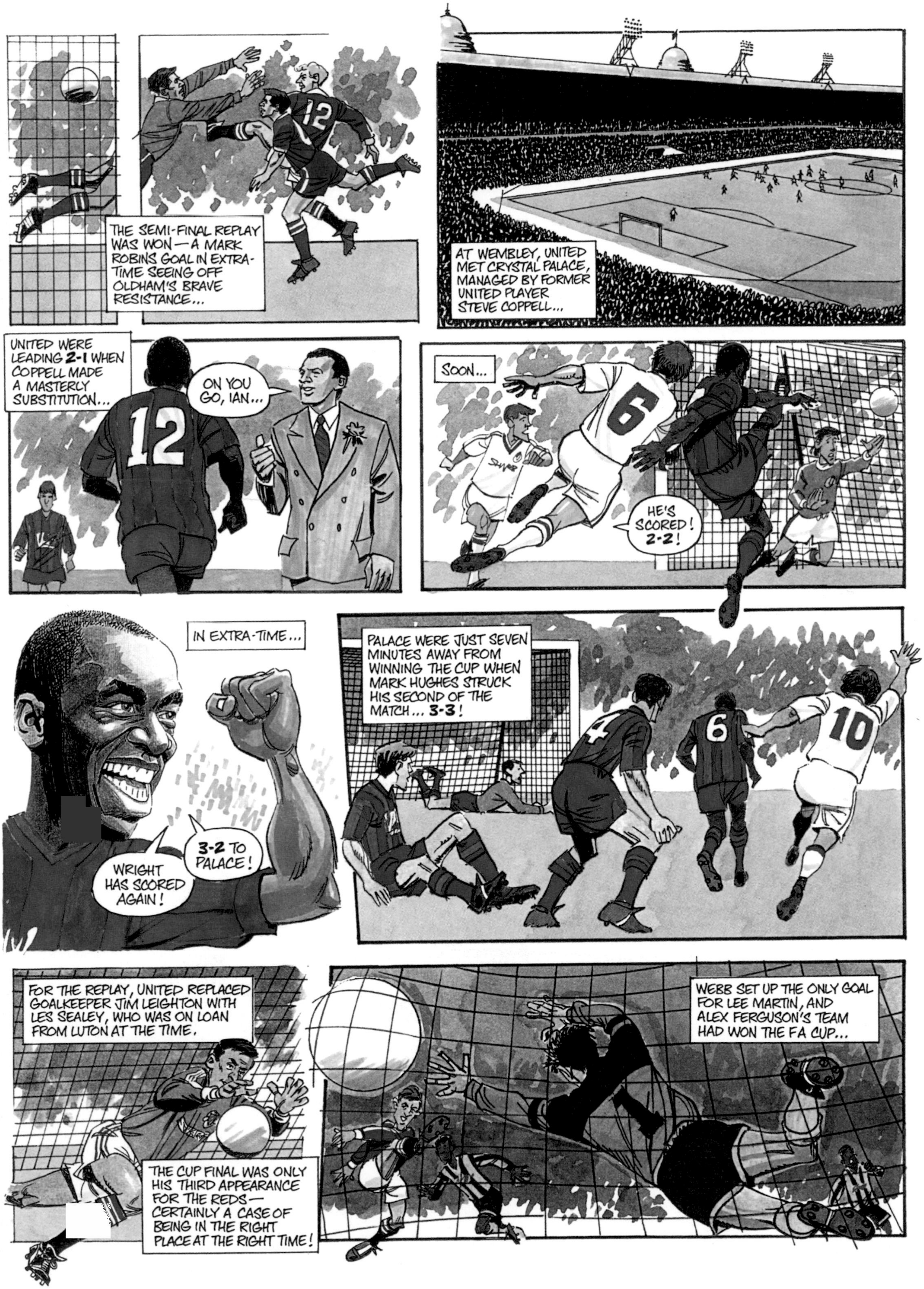

THE SEMI-FINAL REPLAY WAS WON — A MARK ROBINS GOAL IN EXTRA-TIME SEEING OFF OLDHAM'S BRAVE RESISTANCE...
AT WEMBLEY, UNITED MET CRYSTAL PALACE, MANAGED BY FORMER UNITED PLAYER STEVE COPPELL...
UNITED WERE LEADING **2-1** WHEN COPPELL MADE A MASTERLY SUBSTITUTION...
ON YOU GO, IAN...
SOON...
HE'S SCORED! **2-2**!
IN EXTRA-TIME...
3-2 TO PALACE!
WRIGHT HAS SCORED AGAIN!
PALACE WERE JUST SEVEN MINUTES AWAY FROM WINNING THE CUP WHEN MARK HUGHES STRUCK HIS SECOND OF THE MATCH... **3-3**!
FOR THE REPLAY, UNITED REPLACED GOALKEEPER JIM LEIGHTON WITH LES SEALEY, WHO WAS ON LOAN FROM LUTON AT THE TIME.
THE CUP FINAL WAS ONLY HIS THIRD APPEARANCE FOR THE REDS — CERTAINLY A CASE OF BEING IN THE RIGHT PLACE AT THE RIGHT TIME!
WEBB SET UP THE ONLY GOAL FOR LEE MARTIN, AND ALEX FERGUSON'S TEAM HAD WON THE FA CUP...

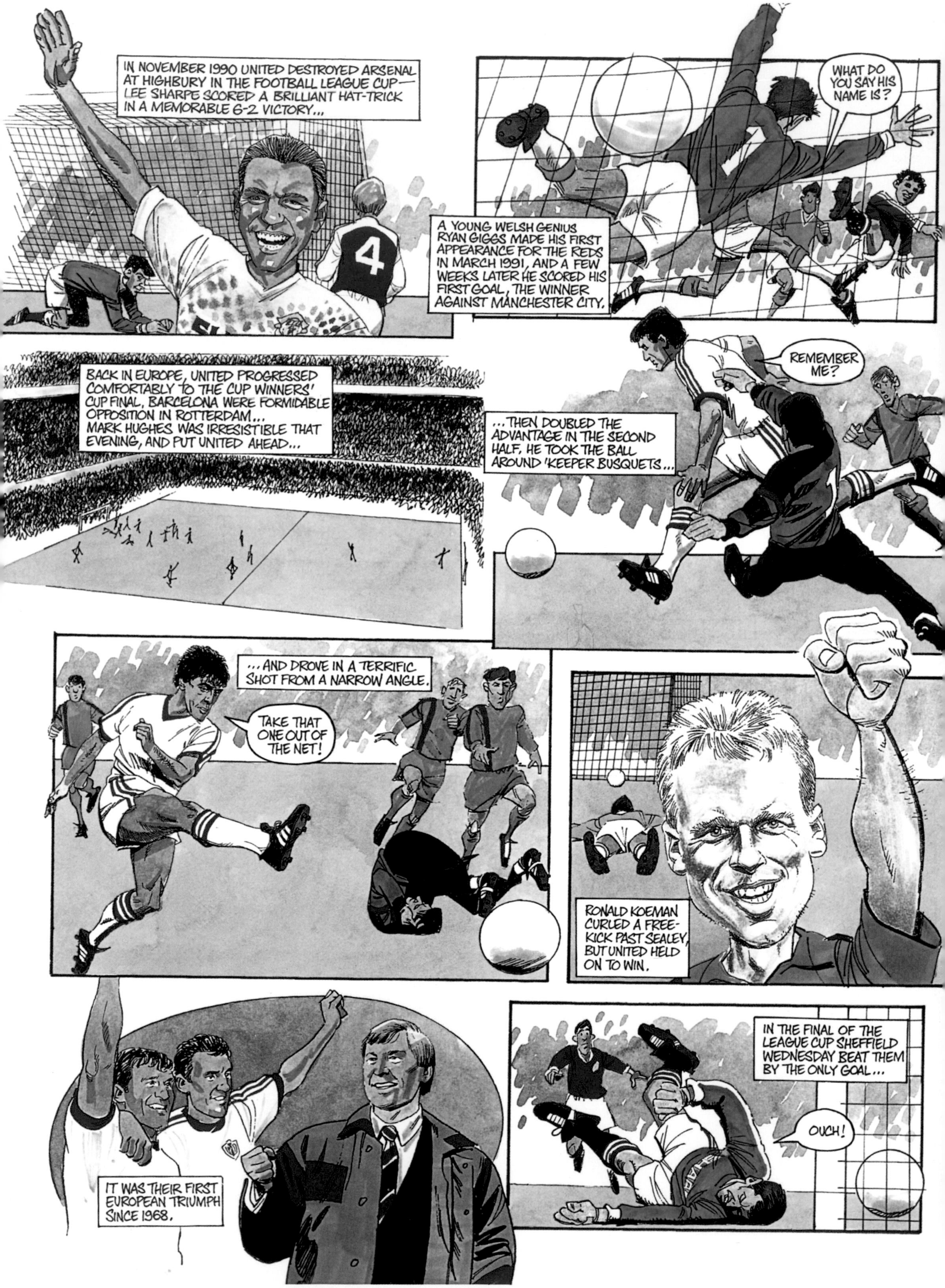
IN NOVEMBER 1990 UNITED DESTROYED ARSENAL AT HIGHBURY IN THE FOOTBALL LEAGUE CUP — LEE SHARPE SCORED A BRILLIANT HAT-TRICK IN A MEMORABLE 6-2 VICTORY...
A YOUNG WELSH GENIUS RYAN GIGGS MADE HIS FIRST APPEARANCE FOR THE REDS IN MARCH 1991, AND A FEW WEEKS LATER HE SCORED HIS FIRST GOAL, THE WINNER AGAINST MANCHESTER CITY.
WHAT DO YOU SAY HIS NAME IS?
BACK IN EUROPE, UNITED PROGRESSED COMFORTABLY TO THE CUP WINNERS' CUP FINAL, BARCELONA WERE FORMIDABLE OPPOSITION IN ROTTERDAM... MARK HUGHES WAS IRRESISTIBLE THAT EVENING, AND PUT UNITED AHEAD...
...THEN DOUBLED THE ADVANTAGE IN THE SECOND HALF, HE TOOK THE BALL AROUND 'KEEPER BUSQUETS...
REMEMBER ME?
...AND DROVE IN A TERRIFIC SHOT FROM A NARROW ANGLE.
TAKE THAT ONE OUT OF THE NET!
RONALD KOEMAN CURLED A FREE-KICK PAST SEALEY, BUT UNITED HELD ON TO WIN.
IT WAS THEIR FIRST EUROPEAN TRIUMPH SINCE 1968.
IN THE FINAL OF THE LEAGUE CUP SHEFFIELD WEDNESDAY BEAT THEM BY THE ONLY GOAL...
OUCH!

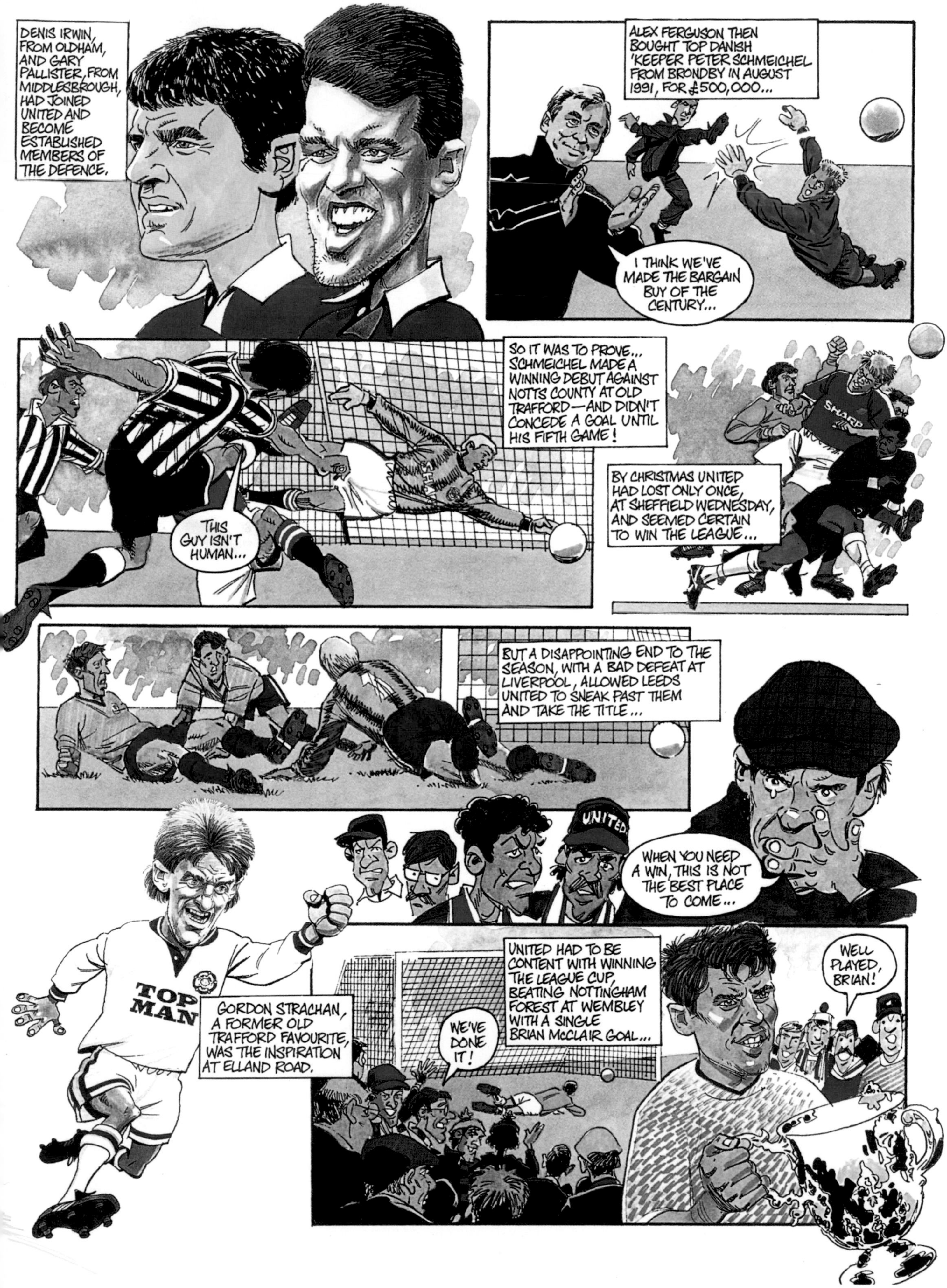
DENIS IRWIN, FROM OLDHAM, AND GARY PALLISTER, FROM MIDDLESBROUGH, HAD JOINED UNITED AND BECOME ESTABLISHED MEMBERS OF THE DEFENCE.
ALEX FERGUSON THEN BOUGHT TOP DANISH 'KEEPER PETER SCHMEICHEL FROM BRONDBY IN AUGUST 1991, FOR £500,000...
I THINK WE'VE MADE THE BARGAIN BUY OF THE CENTURY...
SO IT WAS TO PROVE... SCHMEICHEL MADE A WINNING DEBUT AGAINST NOTTS COUNTY AT OLD TRAFFORD—AND DIDN'T CONCEDE A GOAL UNTIL HIS FIFTH GAME!
THIS GUY ISN'T HUMAN...
SHARP
BY CHRISTMAS UNITED HAD LOST ONLY ONCE, AT SHEFFIELD WEDNESDAY, AND SEEMED CERTAIN TO WIN THE LEAGUE...
BUT A DISAPPOINTING END TO THE SEASON, WITH A BAD DEFEAT AT LIVERPOOL, ALLOWED LEEDS UNITED TO SNEAK PAST THEM AND TAKE THE TITLE...
UNITED
WHEN YOU NEED A WIN, THIS IS NOT THE BEST PLACE TO COME...
TOP MAN
GORDON STRACHAN, A FORMER OLD TRAFFORD FAVOURITE, WAS THE INSPIRATION AT ELLAND ROAD.
UNITED HAD TO BE CONTENT WITH WINNING THE LEAGUE CUP, BEATING NOTTINGHAM FOREST AT WEMBLEY WITH A SINGLE BRIAN McCLAIR GOAL...
WE'VE DONE IT!
WELL PLAYED, BRIAN!

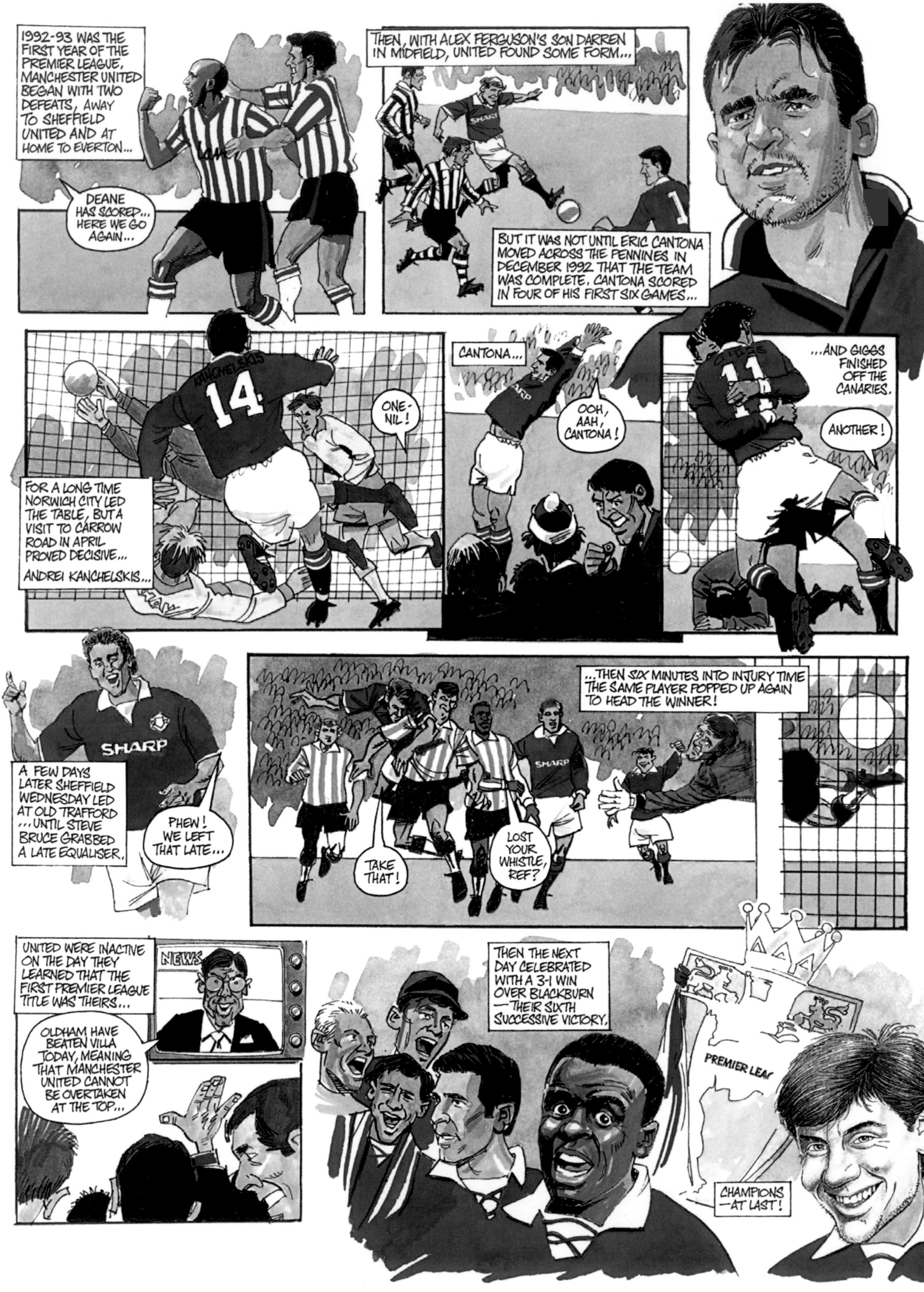
1992-93 WAS THE FIRST YEAR OF THE PREMIER LEAGUE. MANCHESTER UNITED BEGAN WITH TWO DEFEATS, AWAY TO SHEFFIELD UNITED AND AT HOME TO EVERTON...
DEANE HAS SCORED... HERE WE GO AGAIN...
THEN, WITH ALEX FERGUSON'S SON DARREN IN MIDFIELD, UNITED FOUND SOME FORM...
BUT IT WAS NOT UNTIL ERIC CANTONA MOVED ACROSS THE PENNINES IN DECEMBER 1992 THAT THE TEAM WAS COMPLETE. CANTONA SCORED IN FOUR OF HIS FIRST SIX GAMES...
FOR A LONG TIME NORWICH CITY LED THE TABLE, BUT A VISIT TO CARROW ROAD IN APRIL PROVED DECISIVE...
ANDREI KANCHELSKIS...
ONE-NIL!
CANTONA...
OOH, AAH, CANTONA!
...AND GIGGS FINISHED OFF THE CANARIES.
ANOTHER!
A FEW DAYS LATER SHEFFIELD WEDNESDAY LED AT OLD TRAFFORD ...UNTIL STEVE BRUCE GRABBED A LATE EQUALISER.
PHEW! WE LEFT THAT LATE...
...THEN SIX MINUTES INTO INJURY TIME THE SAME PLAYER POPPED UP AGAIN TO HEAD THE WINNER!
TAKE THAT!
LOST YOUR WHISTLE, REF?
UNITED WERE INACTIVE ON THE DAY THEY LEARNED THAT THE FIRST PREMIER LEAGUE TITLE WAS THEIRS...
NEWS
OLDHAM HAVE BEATEN VILLA TODAY, MEANING THAT MANCHESTER UNITED CANNOT BE OVERTAKEN AT THE TOP...
THEN THE NEXT DAY CELEBRATED WITH A 3-1 WIN OVER BLACKBURN —THEIR SIXTH SUCCESSIVE VICTORY.
PREMIER LEA
CHAMPIONS —AT LAST!

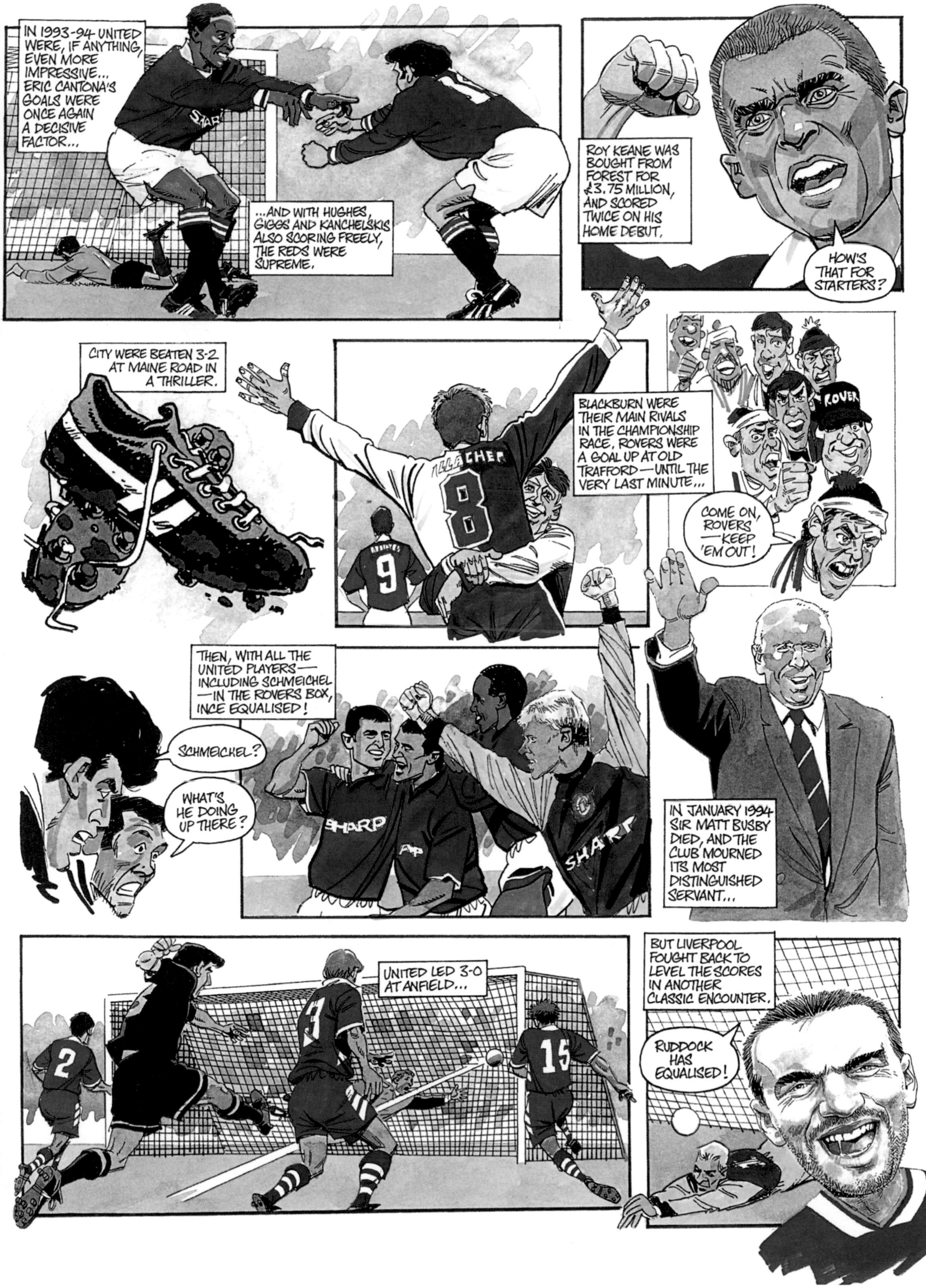
IN 1993-94 UNITED WERE, IF ANYTHING, EVEN MORE IMPRESSIVE... ERIC CANTONA'S GOALS WERE ONCE AGAIN A DECISIVE FACTOR...
...AND WITH HUGHES, GIGGS AND KANCHELSKIS ALSO SCORING FREELY, THE REDS WERE SUPREME.
ROY KEANE WAS BOUGHT FROM FOREST FOR £3.75 MILLION, AND SCORED TWICE ON HIS HOME DEBUT.
HOW'S THAT FOR STARTERS?
CITY WERE BEATEN 3-2 AT MAINE ROAD IN A THRILLER.
BLACKBURN WERE THEIR MAIN RIVALS IN THE CHAMPIONSHIP RACE. ROVERS WERE A GOAL UP AT OLD TRAFFORD — UNTIL THE VERY LAST MINUTE...
ROVER
COME ON, ROVERS — KEEP 'EM OUT!
THEN, WITH ALL THE UNITED PLAYERS — INCLUDING SCHMEICHEL — IN THE ROVERS BOX, INCE EQUALISED!
SCHMEICHEL?
WHAT'S HE DOING UP THERE?
IN JANUARY 1994 SIR MATT BUSBY DIED, AND THE CLUB MOURNED ITS MOST DISTINGUISHED SERVANT...
UNITED LED 3-0 AT ANFIELD...
BUT LIVERPOOL FOUGHT BACK TO LEVEL THE SCORES IN ANOTHER CLASSIC ENCOUNTER.
RUDDOCK HAS EQUALISED!

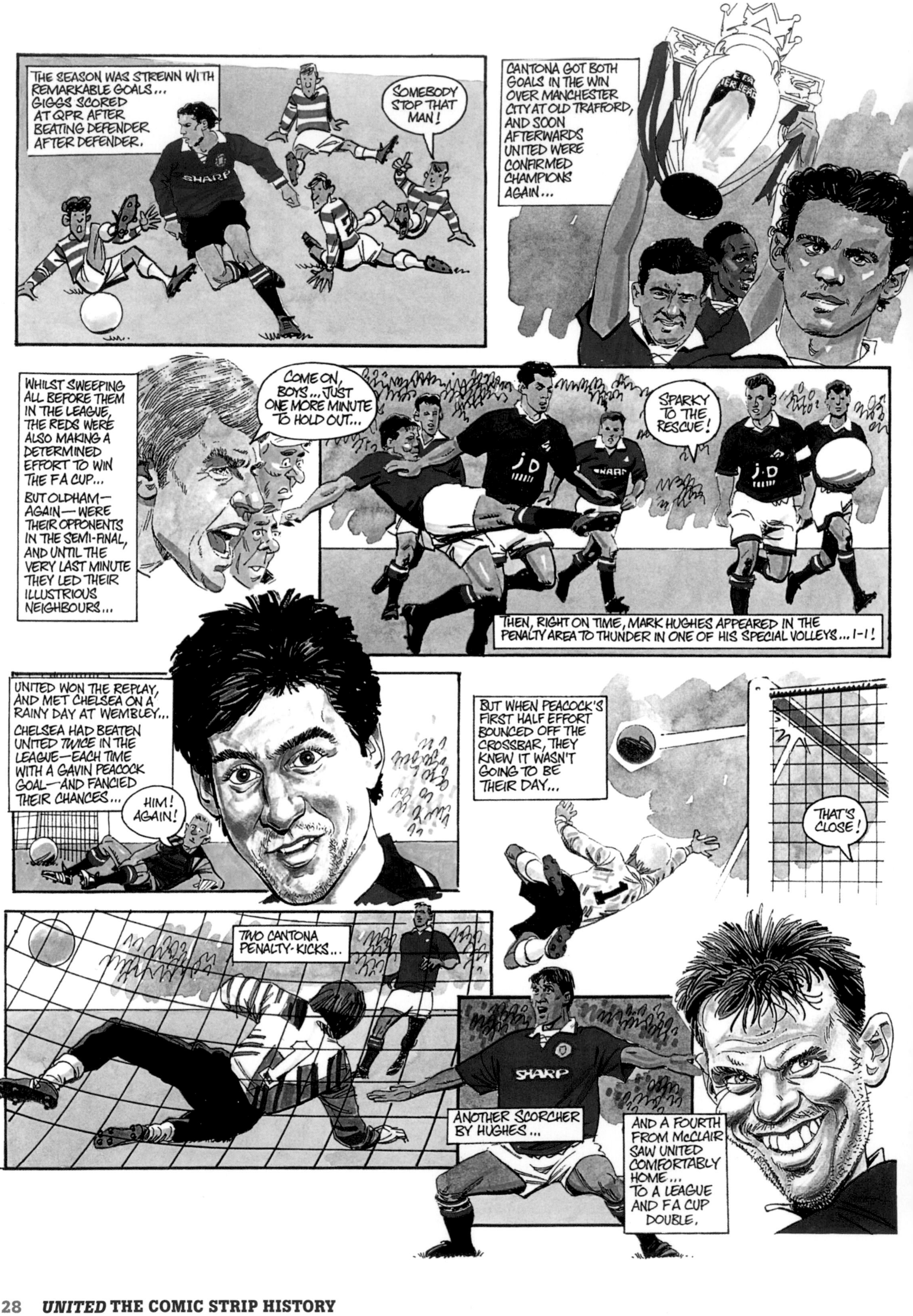
THE SEASON WAS STREWN WITH REMARKABLE GOALS... GIGGS SCORED AT QPR AFTER BEATING DEFENDER AFTER DEFENDER.
SOMEBODY STOP THAT MAN!
SHARP
CANTONA GOT BOTH GOALS IN THE WIN OVER MANCHESTER CITY AT OLD TRAFFORD, AND SOON AFTERWARDS UNITED WERE CONFIRMED CHAMPIONS AGAIN...
WHILST SWEEPING ALL BEFORE THEM IN THE LEAGUE, THE REDS WERE ALSO MAKING A DETERMINED EFFORT TO WIN THE FA CUP...
BUT OLDHAM—AGAIN—WERE THEIR OPPONENTS IN THE SEMI-FINAL, AND UNTIL THE VERY LAST MINUTE THEY LED THEIR ILLUSTRIOUS NEIGHBOURS...
COME ON, BOYS... JUST ONE MORE MINUTE TO HOLD OUT...
SPARKY TO THE RESCUE!
THEN, RIGHT ON TIME, MARK HUGHES APPEARED IN THE PENALTY AREA TO THUNDER IN ONE OF HIS SPECIAL VOLLEYS... 1-1!
UNITED WON THE REPLAY, AND MET CHELSEA ON A RAINY DAY AT WEMBLEY...
CHELSEA HAD BEATEN UNITED TWICE IN THE LEAGUE—EACH TIME WITH A GAVIN PEACOCK GOAL—AND FANCIED THEIR CHANCES...
HIM! AGAIN!
BUT WHEN PEACOCK'S FIRST HALF EFFORT BOUNCED OFF THE CROSSBAR, THEY KNEW IT WASN'T GOING TO BE THEIR DAY...
THAT'S CLOSE!
TWO CANTONA PENALTY-KICKS...
SHARP
ANOTHER SCORCHER BY HUGHES...
AND A FOURTH FROM McCLAIR SAW UNITED COMFORTABLY HOME... TO A LEAGUE AND FA CUP DOUBLE.

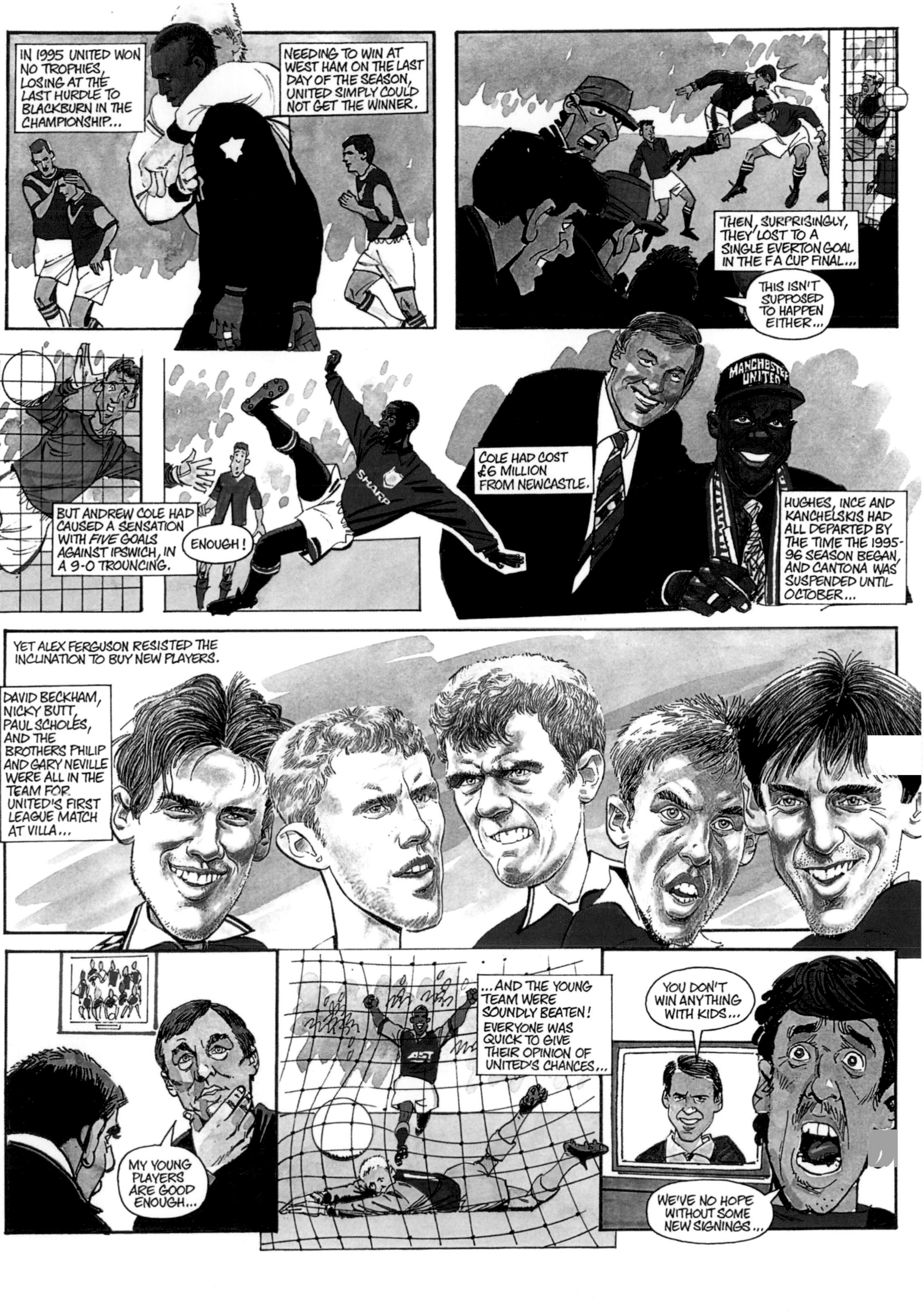
IN 1995 UNITED WON NO TROPHIES, LOSING AT THE LAST HURDLE TO BLACKBURN IN THE CHAMPIONSHIP...
NEEDING TO WIN AT WEST HAM ON THE LAST DAY OF THE SEASON, UNITED SIMPLY COULD NOT GET THE WINNER.
THEN, SURPRISINGLY, THEY LOST TO A SINGLE EVERTON GOAL IN THE FA CUP FINAL...
THIS ISN'T SUPPOSED TO HAPPEN EITHER...
BUT ANDREW COLE HAD CAUSED A SENSATION WITH *FIVE* GOALS AGAINST IPSWICH, IN A 9-0 TROUNCING.
ENOUGH!
SHARP
COLE HAD COST £6 MILLION FROM NEWCASTLE.
MANCHESTER UNITED
HUGHES, INCE AND KANCHELSKIS HAD ALL DEPARTED BY THE TIME THE 1995-96 SEASON BEGAN, AND CANTONA WAS SUSPENDED UNTIL OCTOBER...
YET ALEX FERGUSON RESISTED THE INCLINATION TO BUY NEW PLAYERS.
DAVID BECKHAM, NICKY BUTT, PAUL SCHOLES, AND THE BROTHERS PHILIP AND GARY NEVILLE WERE ALL IN THE TEAM FOR UNITED'S FIRST LEAGUE MATCH AT VILLA...
MY YOUNG PLAYERS ARE GOOD ENOUGH...
...AND THE YOUNG TEAM WERE SOUNDLY BEATEN! EVERYONE WAS QUICK TO GIVE THEIR OPINION OF UNITED'S CHANCES...
AST
YOU DON'T WIN ANYTHING WITH KIDS...
WE'VE NO HOPE WITHOUT SOME NEW SIGNINGS...

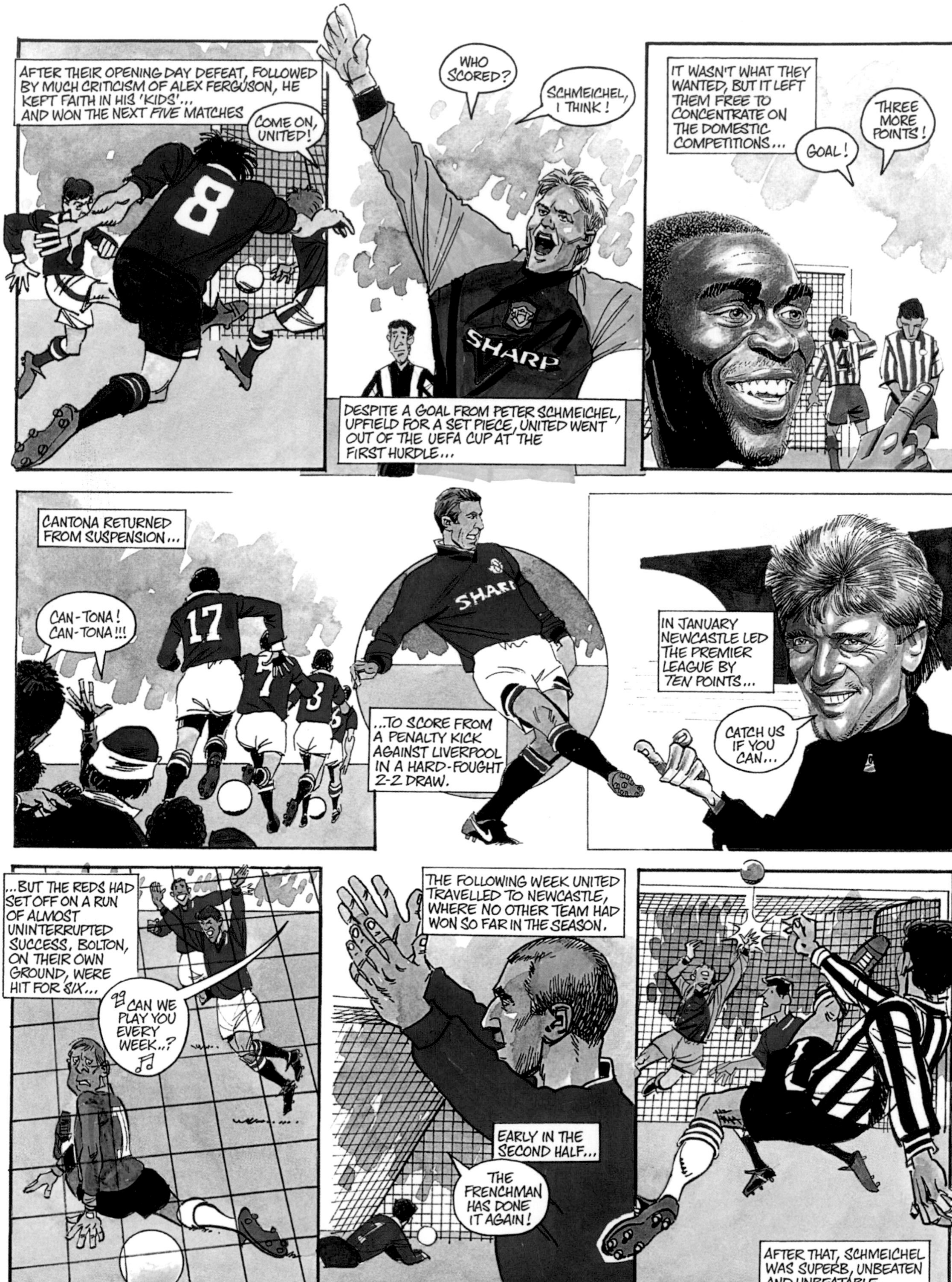

AFTER THEIR OPENING DAY DEFEAT, FOLLOWED BY MUCH CRITICISM OF ALEX FERGUSON, HE KEPT FAITH IN HIS 'KIDS'... AND WON THE NEXT FIVE MATCHES
COME ON, UNITED!
WHO SCORED?
SCHMEICHEL, I THINK!
DESPITE A GOAL FROM PETER SCHMEICHEL, UPFIELD FOR A SET PIECE, UNITED WENT OUT OF THE UEFA CUP AT THE FIRST HURDLE...
IT WASN'T WHAT THEY WANTED, BUT IT LEFT THEM FREE TO CONCENTRATE ON THE DOMESTIC COMPETITIONS...
GOAL!
THREE MORE POINTS!
CANTONA RETURNED FROM SUSPENSION...
CAN-TONA! CAN-TONA!!!
...TO SCORE FROM A PENALTY KICK AGAINST LIVERPOOL IN A HARD-FOUGHT 2-2 DRAW.
IN JANUARY NEWCASTLE LED THE PREMIER LEAGUE BY TEN POINTS...
CATCH US IF YOU CAN...
...BUT THE REDS HAD SET OFF ON A RUN OF ALMOST UNINTERRUPTED SUCCESS. BOLTON, ON THEIR OWN GROUND, WERE HIT FOR SIX...
CAN WE PLAY YOU EVERY WEEK..?
THE FOLLOWING WEEK UNITED TRAVELLED TO NEWCASTLE, WHERE NO OTHER TEAM HAD WON SO FAR IN THE SEASON.
EARLY IN THE SECOND HALF...
THE FRENCHMAN HAS DONE IT AGAIN!
AFTER THAT, SCHMEICHEL WAS SUPERB, UNBEATEN AND UNBEATABLE.

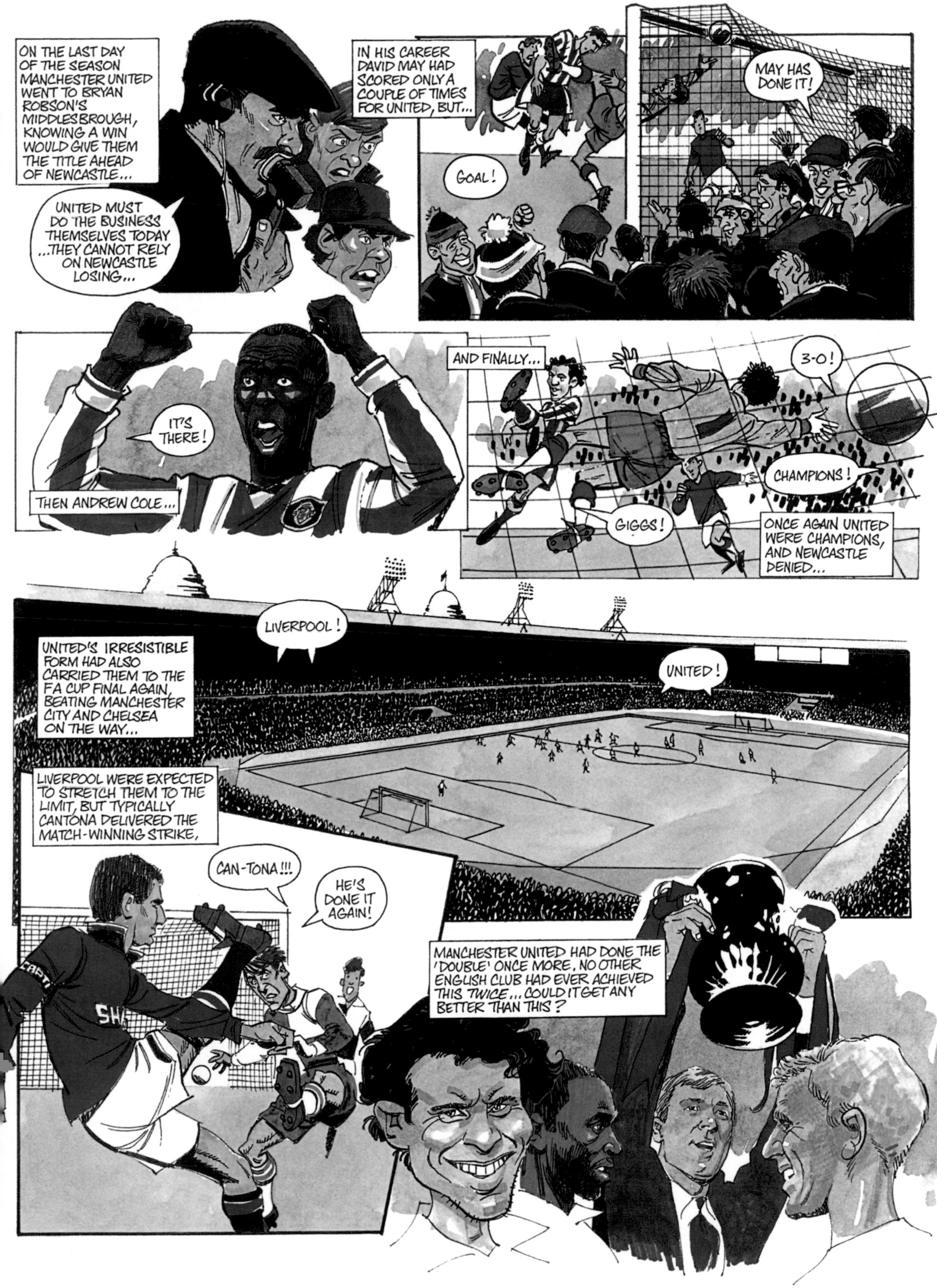
ON THE LAST DAY OF THE SEASON MANCHESTER UNITED WENT TO BRYAN ROBSON'S MIDDLESBROUGH, KNOWING A WIN WOULD GIVE THEM THE TITLE AHEAD OF NEWCASTLE...
UNITED MUST DO THE BUSINESS THEMSELVES TODAY ...THEY CANNOT RELY ON NEWCASTLE LOSING...
IN HIS CAREER DAVID MAY HAD SCORED ONLY A COUPLE OF TIMES FOR UNITED, BUT...
GOAL!
MAY HAS DONE IT!
IT'S THERE!
THEN ANDREW COLE...
AND FINALLY...
3-0!
CHAMPIONS!
GIGGS!
ONCE AGAIN UNITED WERE CHAMPIONS, AND NEWCASTLE DENIED...
LIVERPOOL!
UNITED!
UNITED'S IRRESISTIBLE FORM HAD ALSO CARRIED THEM TO THE FA CUP FINAL AGAIN, BEATING MANCHESTER CITY AND CHELSEA ON THE WAY...
LIVERPOOL WERE EXPECTED TO STRETCH THEM TO THE LIMIT, BUT TYPICALLY CANTONA DELIVERED THE MATCH-WINNING STRIKE,
CAN-TONA!!!
HE'S DONE IT AGAIN!
MANCHESTER UNITED HAD DONE THE 'DOUBLE' ONCE MORE, NO OTHER ENGLISH CLUB HAD EVER ACHIEVED THIS *TWICE*... COULD IT GET ANY BETTER THAN THIS?

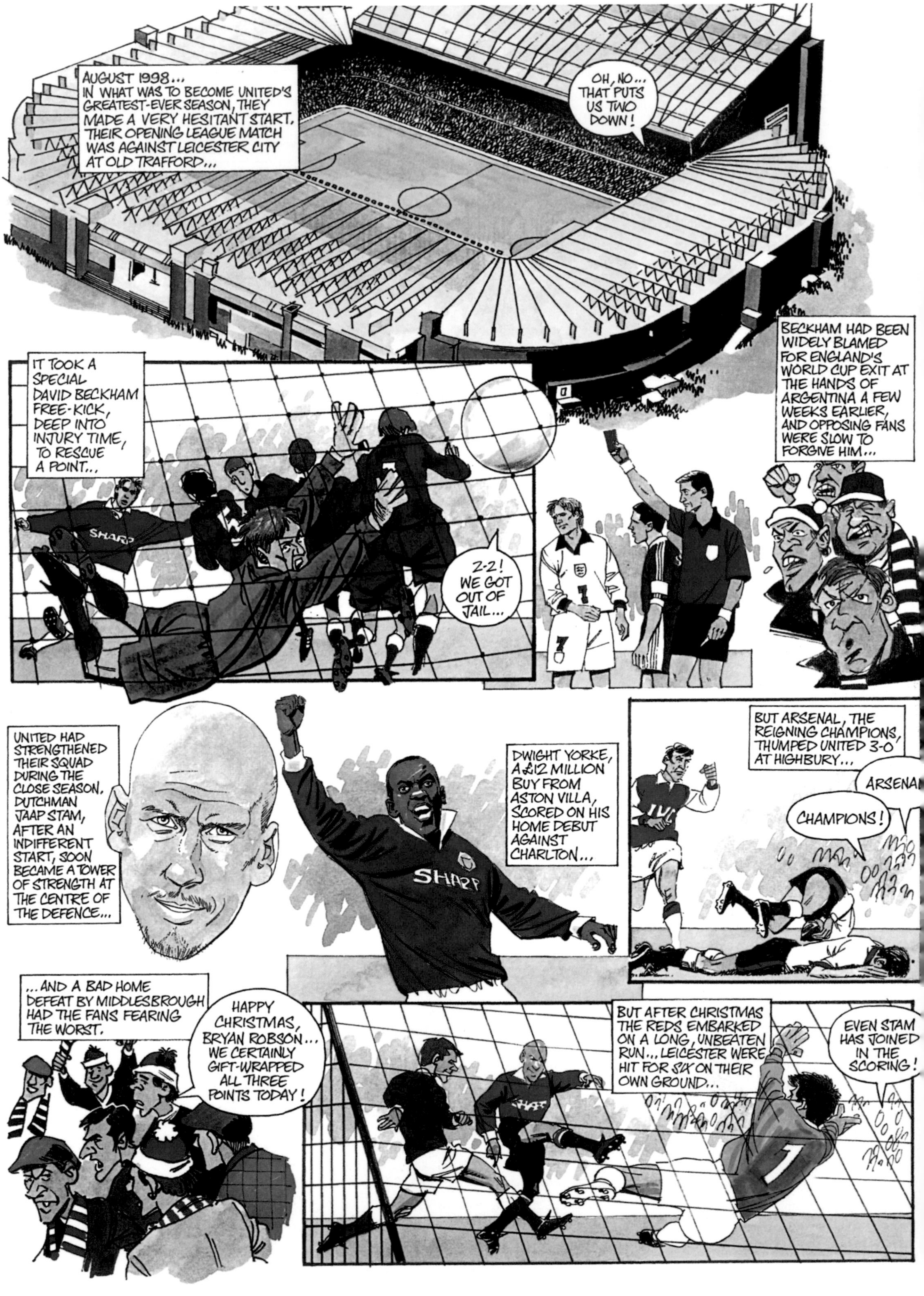
AUGUST 1998... IN WHAT WAS TO BECOME UNITED'S GREATEST-EVER SEASON, THEY MADE A VERY HESITANT START. THEIR OPENING LEAGUE MATCH WAS AGAINST LEICESTER CITY AT OLD TRAFFORD...
OH, NO... THAT PUTS US TWO DOWN!
IT TOOK A SPECIAL DAVID BECKHAM FREE-KICK, DEEP INTO INJURY TIME, TO RESCUE A POINT...
SHARP
2-2! WE GOT OUT OF JAIL...
BECKHAM HAD BEEN WIDELY BLAMED FOR ENGLAND'S WORLD CUP EXIT AT THE HANDS OF ARGENTINA A FEW WEEKS EARLIER, AND OPPOSING FANS WERE SLOW TO FORGIVE HIM...
UNITED HAD STRENGTHENED THEIR SQUAD DURING THE CLOSE SEASON. DUTCHMAN JAAP STAM, AFTER AN INDIFFERENT START, SOON BECAME A TOWER OF STRENGTH AT THE CENTRE OF THE DEFENCE...
DWIGHT YORKE, A £12 MILLION BUY FROM ASTON VILLA, SCORED ON HIS HOME DEBUT AGAINST CHARLTON...
SHARP
BUT ARSENAL, THE REIGNING CHAMPIONS, THUMPED UNITED 3-0 AT HIGHBURY...
ARSENA
CHAMPIONS!
...AND A BAD HOME DEFEAT BY MIDDLESBROUGH HAD THE FANS FEARING THE WORST.
HAPPY CHRISTMAS, BRYAN ROBSON... WE CERTAINLY GIFT-WRAPPED ALL THREE POINTS TODAY!
BUT AFTER CHRISTMAS THE REDS EMBARKED ON A LONG, UNBEATEN RUN... LEICESTER WERE HIT FOR SIX ON THEIR OWN GROUND...
EVEN STAM HAS JOINED IN THE SCORING!

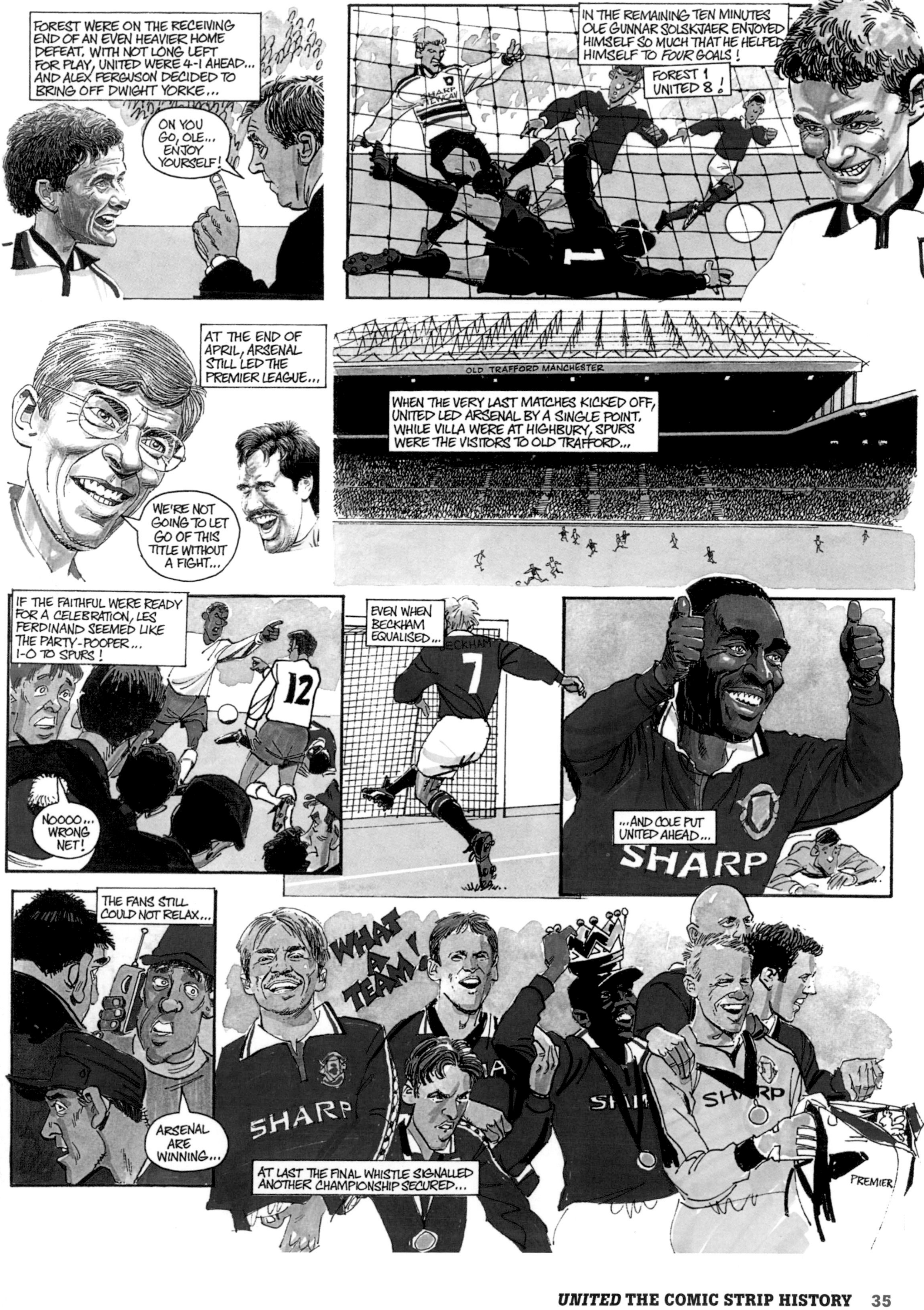
FOREST WERE ON THE RECEIVING END OF AN EVEN HEAVIER HOME DEFEAT. WITH NOT LONG LEFT FOR PLAY, UNITED WERE 4-1 AHEAD... AND ALEX FERGUSON DECIDED TO BRING OFF DWIGHT YORKE...
ON YOU GO, OLE... ENJOY YOURSELF!
IN THE REMAINING TEN MINUTES OLE GUNNAR SOLSKJAER ENJOYED HIMSELF SO MUCH THAT HE HELPED HIMSELF TO *FOUR* GOALS!
FOREST 1 UNITED 8!
AT THE END OF APRIL, ARSENAL STILL LED THE PREMIER LEAGUE...
WE'RE NOT GOING TO LET GO OF THIS TITLE WITHOUT A FIGHT...
OLD TRAFFORD MANCHESTER
WHEN THE VERY LAST MATCHES KICKED OFF, UNITED LED ARSENAL BY A SINGLE POINT. WHILE VILLA WERE AT HIGHBURY, SPURS WERE THE VISITORS TO OLD TRAFFORD...
IF THE FAITHFUL WERE READY FOR A CELEBRATION, LES FERDINAND SEEMED LIKE THE PARTY-POOPER... 1-0 TO SPURS!
NOOOO... WRONG NET!
EVEN WHEN BECKHAM EQUALISED...
...AND COLE PUT UNITED AHEAD...
THE FANS STILL COULD NOT RELAX...
ARSENAL ARE WINNING...
WHAT A TEAM!
AT LAST THE FINAL WHISTLE SIGNALLED ANOTHER CHAMPIONSHIP SECURED...
PREMIER

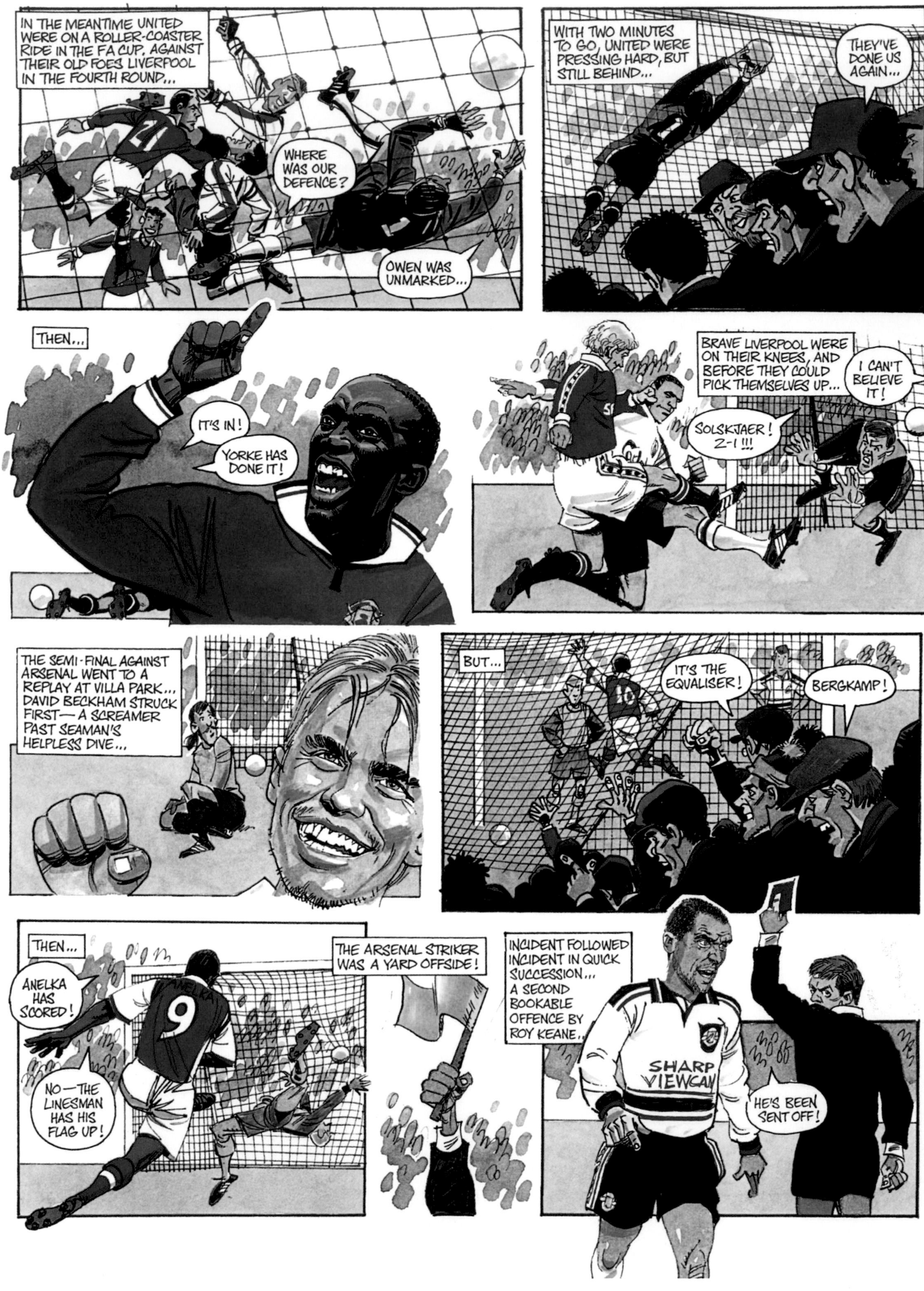

IN THE MEANTIME UNITED WERE ON A ROLLER-COASTER RIDE IN THE FA CUP, AGAINST THEIR OLD FOES LIVERPOOL IN THE FOURTH ROUND...
WHERE WAS OUR DEFENCE?
OWEN WAS UNMARKED...
WITH TWO MINUTES TO GO, UNITED WERE PRESSING HARD, BUT STILL BEHIND...
THEY'VE DONE US AGAIN...
THEN...
IT'S IN!
YORKE HAS DONE IT!
BRAVE LIVERPOOL WERE ON THEIR KNEES, AND BEFORE THEY COULD PICK THEMSELVES UP...
I CAN'T BELIEVE IT!
SOLSKJAER! 2-1!!!
THE SEMI-FINAL AGAINST ARSENAL WENT TO A REPLAY AT VILLA PARK... DAVID BECKHAM STRUCK FIRST— A SCREAMER PAST SEAMAN'S HELPLESS DIVE...
BUT...
IT'S THE EQUALISER!
BERGKAMP!
THEN...
ANELKA HAS SCORED!
NO—THE LINESMAN HAS HIS FLAG UP!
THE ARSENAL STRIKER WAS A YARD OFFSIDE!
INCIDENT FOLLOWED INCIDENT IN QUICK SUCCESSION... A SECOND BOOKABLE OFFENCE BY ROY KEANE...
SHARP VIEWCAM
HE'S BEEN SENT OFF!

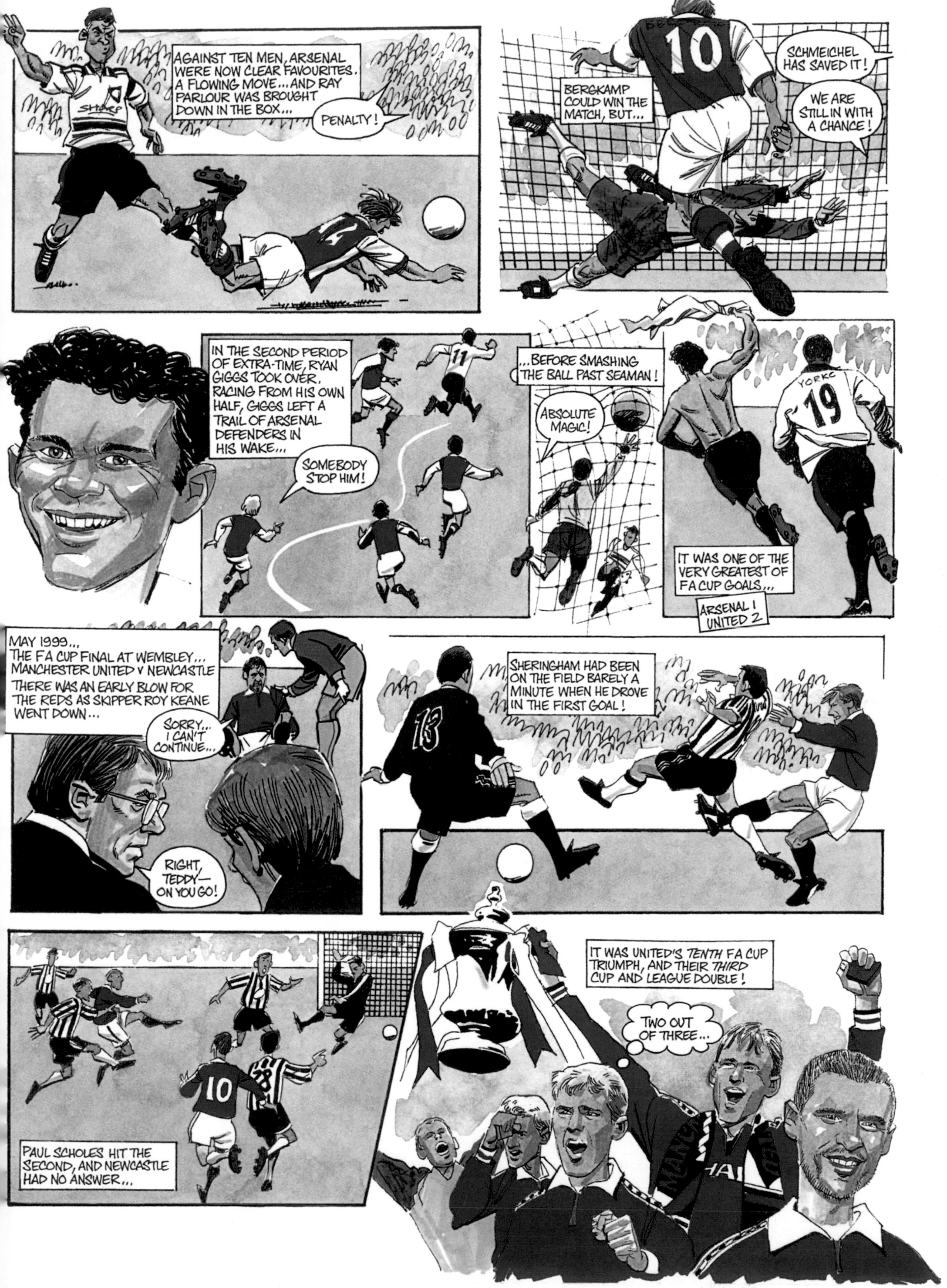

AGAINST TEN MEN, ARSENAL WERE NOW CLEAR FAVOURITES. A FLOWING MOVE... AND RAY PARLOUR WAS BROUGHT DOWN IN THE BOX...
PENALTY!
BERGKAMP COULD WIN THE MATCH, BUT...
SCHMEICHEL HAS SAVED IT!
WE ARE STILL IN WITH A CHANCE!
IN THE SECOND PERIOD OF EXTRA-TIME, RYAN GIGGS TOOK OVER. RACING FROM HIS OWN HALF, GIGGS LEFT A TRAIL OF ARSENAL DEFENDERS IN HIS WAKE...
SOMEBODY STOP HIM!
...BEFORE SMASHING THE BALL PAST SEAMAN!
ABSOLUTE MAGIC!
YORKE
19
IT WAS ONE OF THE VERY GREATEST OF FA CUP GOALS...
ARSENAL 1 UNITED 2
MAY 1999... THE FA CUP FINAL AT WEMBLEY... MANCHESTER UNITED V NEWCASTLE
THERE WAS AN EARLY BLOW FOR THE REDS AS SKIPPER ROY KEANE WENT DOWN...
SORRY... I CAN'T CONTINUE...
RIGHT, TEDDY— ON YOU GO!
SHERINGHAM HAD BEEN ON THE FIELD BARELY A MINUTE WHEN HE DROVE IN THE FIRST GOAL!
PAUL SCHOLES HIT THE SECOND, AND NEWCASTLE HAD NO ANSWER...
IT WAS UNITED'S *TENTH* FA CUP TRIUMPH, AND THEIR *THIRD* CUP AND LEAGUE DOUBLE!
TWO OUT OF THREE...

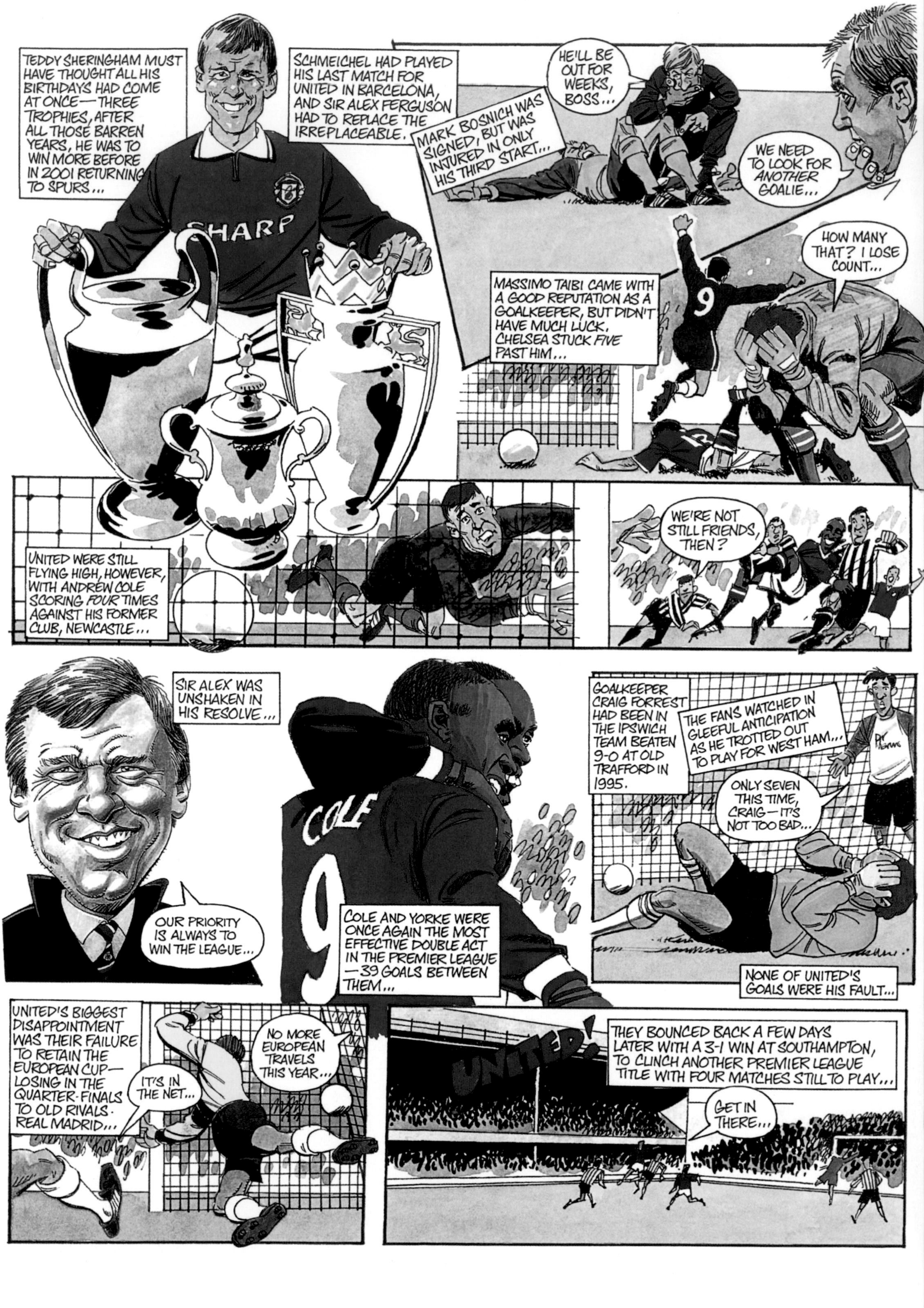
TEDDY SHERINGHAM MUST HAVE THOUGHT ALL HIS BIRTHDAYS HAD COME AT ONCE—THREE TROPHIES, AFTER ALL THOSE BARREN YEARS, HE WAS TO WIN MORE BEFORE IN 2001 RETURNING TO SPURS...
SHARP
SCHMEICHEL HAD PLAYED HIS LAST MATCH FOR UNITED IN BARCELONA, AND SIR ALEX FERGUSON HAD TO REPLACE THE IRREPLACEABLE.
MARK BOSNICH WAS SIGNED, BUT WAS INJURED IN ONLY HIS THIRD START...
HE'LL BE OUT FOR WEEKS, BOSS...
WE NEED TO LOOK FOR ANOTHER GOALIE...
MASSIMO TAIBI CAME WITH A GOOD REPUTATION AS A GOALKEEPER, BUT DIDN'T HAVE MUCH LUCK. CHELSEA STUCK FIVE PAST HIM...
HOW MANY THAT? I LOSE COUNT...
UNITED WERE STILL FLYING HIGH, HOWEVER, WITH ANDREW COLE SCORING FOUR TIMES AGAINST HIS FORMER CLUB, NEWCASTLE...
WE'RE NOT STILL FRIENDS, THEN?
SIR ALEX WAS UNSHAKEN IN HIS RESOLVE...
OUR PRIORITY IS ALWAYS TO WIN THE LEAGUE...
COLE
9
COLE AND YORKE WERE ONCE AGAIN THE MOST EFFECTIVE DOUBLE ACT IN THE PREMIER LEAGUE —39 GOALS BETWEEN THEM...
GOALKEEPER CRAIG FORREST HAD BEEN IN THE IPSWICH TEAM BEATEN 9-0 AT OLD TRAFFORD IN 1995.
THE FANS WATCHED IN GLEEFUL ANTICIPATION AS HE TROTTED OUT TO PLAY FOR WEST HAM...
ONLY SEVEN THIS TIME, CRAIG—IT'S NOT TOO BAD...
NONE OF UNITED'S GOALS WERE HIS FAULT...
UNITED'S BIGGEST DISAPPOINTMENT WAS THEIR FAILURE TO RETAIN THE EUROPEAN CUP—LOSING IN THE QUARTER-FINALS TO OLD RIVALS REAL MADRID...
IT'S IN THE NET...
NO MORE EUROPEAN TRAVELS THIS YEAR...
UNITED!
THEY BOUNCED BACK A FEW DAYS LATER WITH A 3-1 WIN AT SOUTHAMPTON, TO CLINCH ANOTHER PREMIER LEAGUE TITLE WITH FOUR MATCHES STILL TO PLAY...
GET IN THERE...

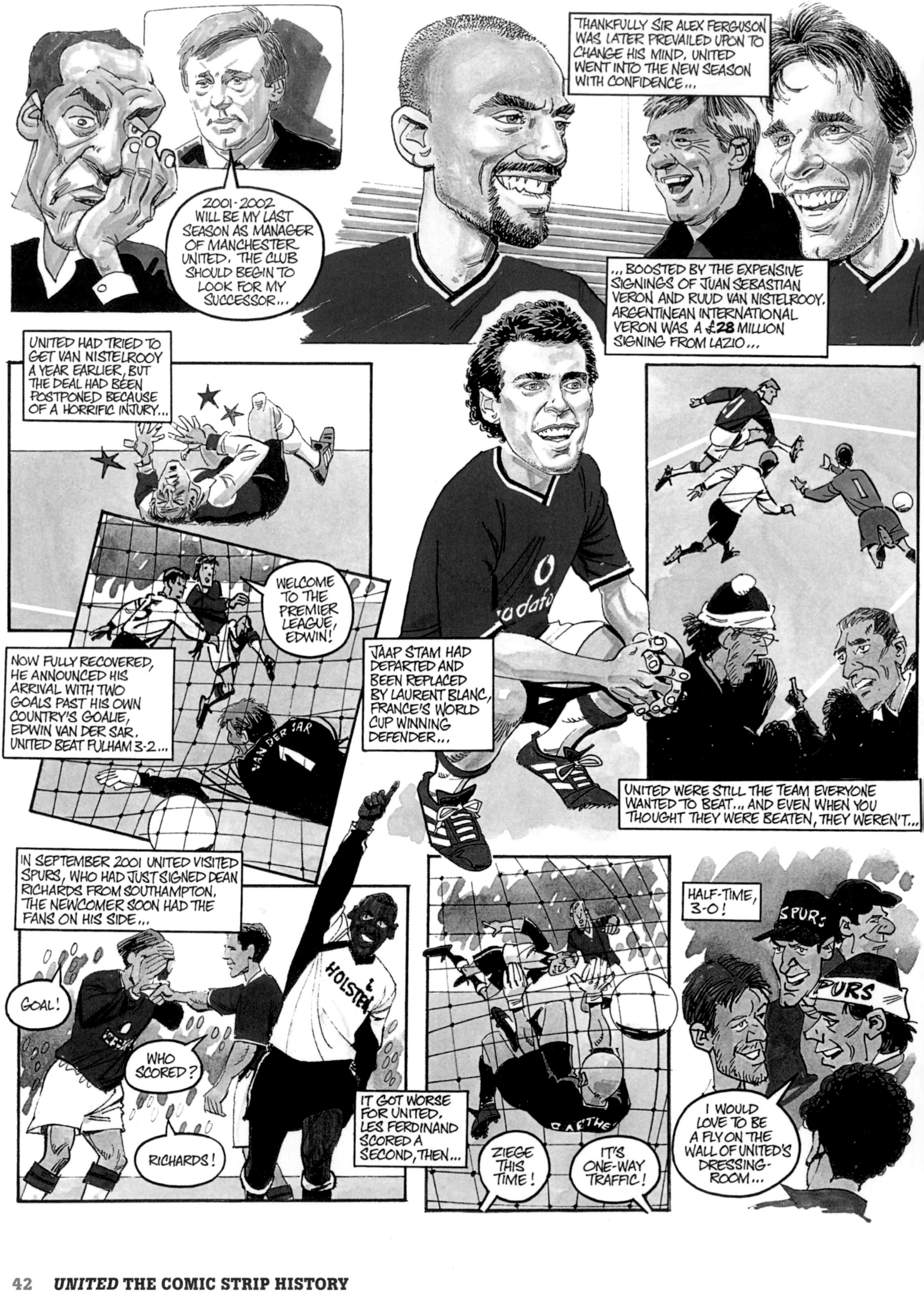
2001-2002 WILL BE MY LAST SEASON AS MANAGER OF MANCHESTER UNITED. THE CLUB SHOULD BEGIN TO LOOK FOR MY SUCCESSOR...
THANKFULLY SIR ALEX FERGUSON WAS LATER PREVAILED UPON TO CHANGE HIS MIND. UNITED WENT INTO THE NEW SEASON WITH CONFIDENCE...
...BOOSTED BY THE EXPENSIVE SIGNINGS OF JUAN SEBASTIAN VERON AND RUUD VAN NISTELROOY. ARGENTINEAN INTERNATIONAL VERON WAS A £28 MILLION SIGNING FROM LAZIO...
UNITED HAD TRIED TO GET VAN NISTELROOY A YEAR EARLIER, BUT THE DEAL HAD BEEN POSTPONED BECAUSE OF A HORRIFIC INJURY...
WELCOME TO THE PREMIER LEAGUE, EDWIN!
NOW FULLY RECOVERED, HE ANNOUNCED HIS ARRIVAL WITH TWO GOALS PAST HIS OWN COUNTRY'S GOALIE, EDWIN VAN DER SAR. UNITED BEAT FULHAM 3-2...
VAN DER SAR
JAAP STAM HAD DEPARTED AND BEEN REPLACED BY LAURENT BLANC, FRANCE'S WORLD CUP WINNING DEFENDER...
UNITED WERE STILL THE TEAM EVERYONE WANTED TO BEAT... AND EVEN WHEN YOU THOUGHT THEY WERE BEATEN, THEY WEREN'T...
IN SEPTEMBER 2001 UNITED VISITED SPURS, WHO HAD JUST SIGNED DEAN RICHARDS FROM SOUTHAMPTON. THE NEWCOMER SOON HAD THE FANS ON HIS SIDE...
GOAL!
WHO SCORED?
RICHARDS!
HOLSTEN
IT GOT WORSE FOR UNITED. LES FERDINAND SCORED A SECOND, THEN...
ZIEGE THIS TIME!
IT'S ONE-WAY TRAFFIC!
HALF-TIME, 3-0!
SPURS
SPURS
I WOULD LOVE TO BE A FLY ON THE WALL OF UNITED'S DRESSING-ROOM...

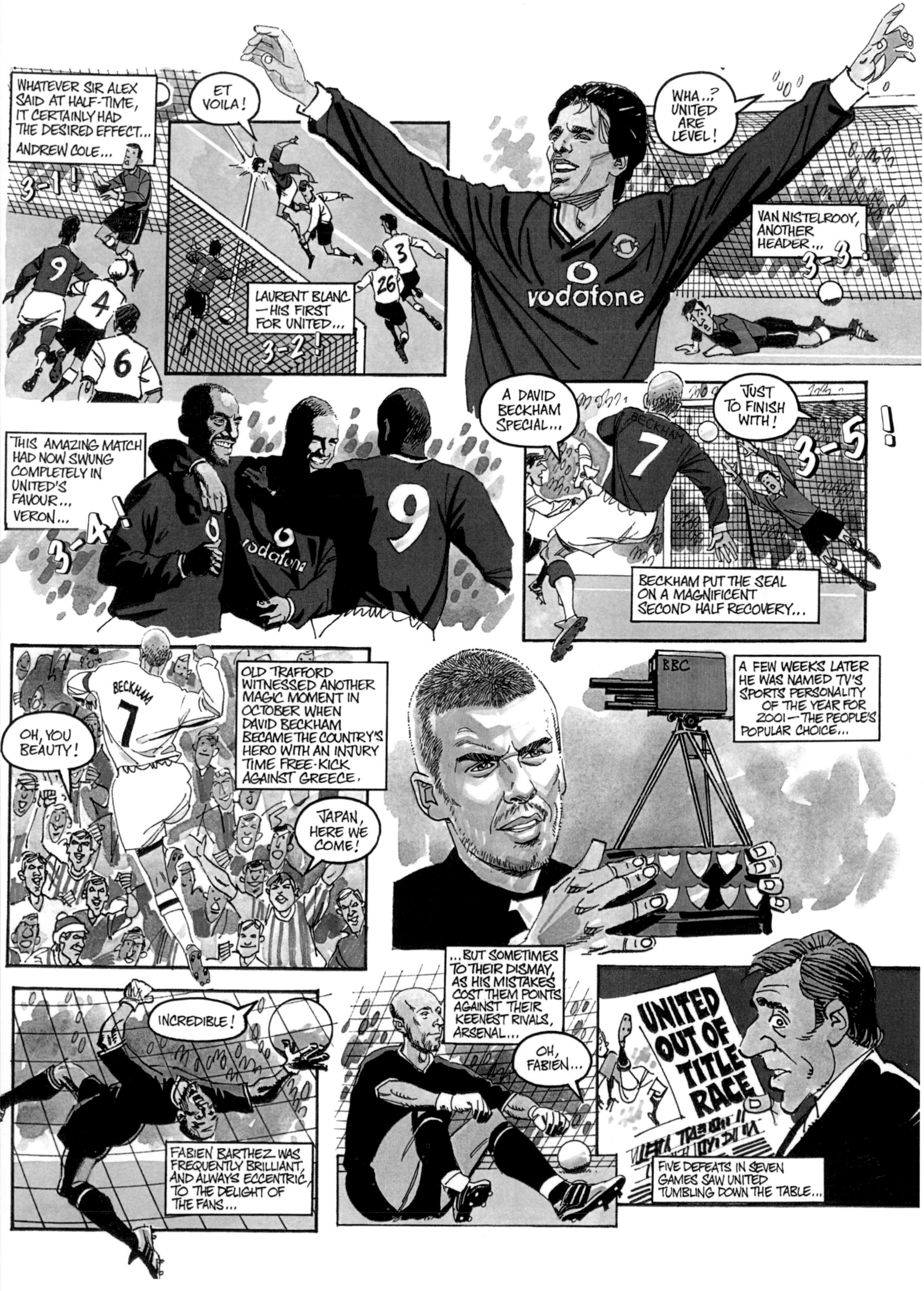
WHATEVER SIR ALEX SAID AT HALF-TIME, IT CERTAINLY HAD THE DESIRED EFFECT... ANDREW COLE...
3-1!
ET VOILA!
LAURENT BLANC — HIS FIRST FOR UNITED...
3-2!
WHA..? UNITED ARE LEVEL!
VAN NISTELROOY, ANOTHER HEADER...
3-3!
THIS AMAZING MATCH HAD NOW SWUNG COMPLETELY IN UNITED'S FAVOUR... VERON...
3-4!
A DAVID BECKHAM SPECIAL...
JUST TO FINISH WITH!
3-5!
BECKHAM PUT THE SEAL ON A MAGNIFICENT SECOND HALF RECOVERY...
OLD TRAFFORD WITNESSED ANOTHER MAGIC MOMENT IN OCTOBER WHEN DAVID BECKHAM BECAME THE COUNTRY'S HERO WITH AN INJURY TIME FREE-KICK AGAINST GREECE.
OH, YOU BEAUTY!
JAPAN, HERE WE COME!
BBC
A FEW WEEKS LATER HE WAS NAMED TV'S SPORTS PERSONALITY OF THE YEAR FOR 2001 — THE PEOPLE'S POPULAR CHOICE...
INCREDIBLE!
FABIEN BARTHEZ WAS FREQUENTLY BRILLIANT, AND ALWAYS ECCENTRIC, TO THE DELIGHT OF THE FANS...
...BUT SOMETIMES TO THEIR DISMAY, AS HIS MISTAKES COST THEM POINTS AGAINST THEIR KEENEST RIVALS, ARSENAL...
OH, FABIEN...
UNITED OUT OF TITLE RACE
FIVE DEFEATS IN SEVEN GAMES SAW UNITED TUMBLING DOWN THE TABLE...

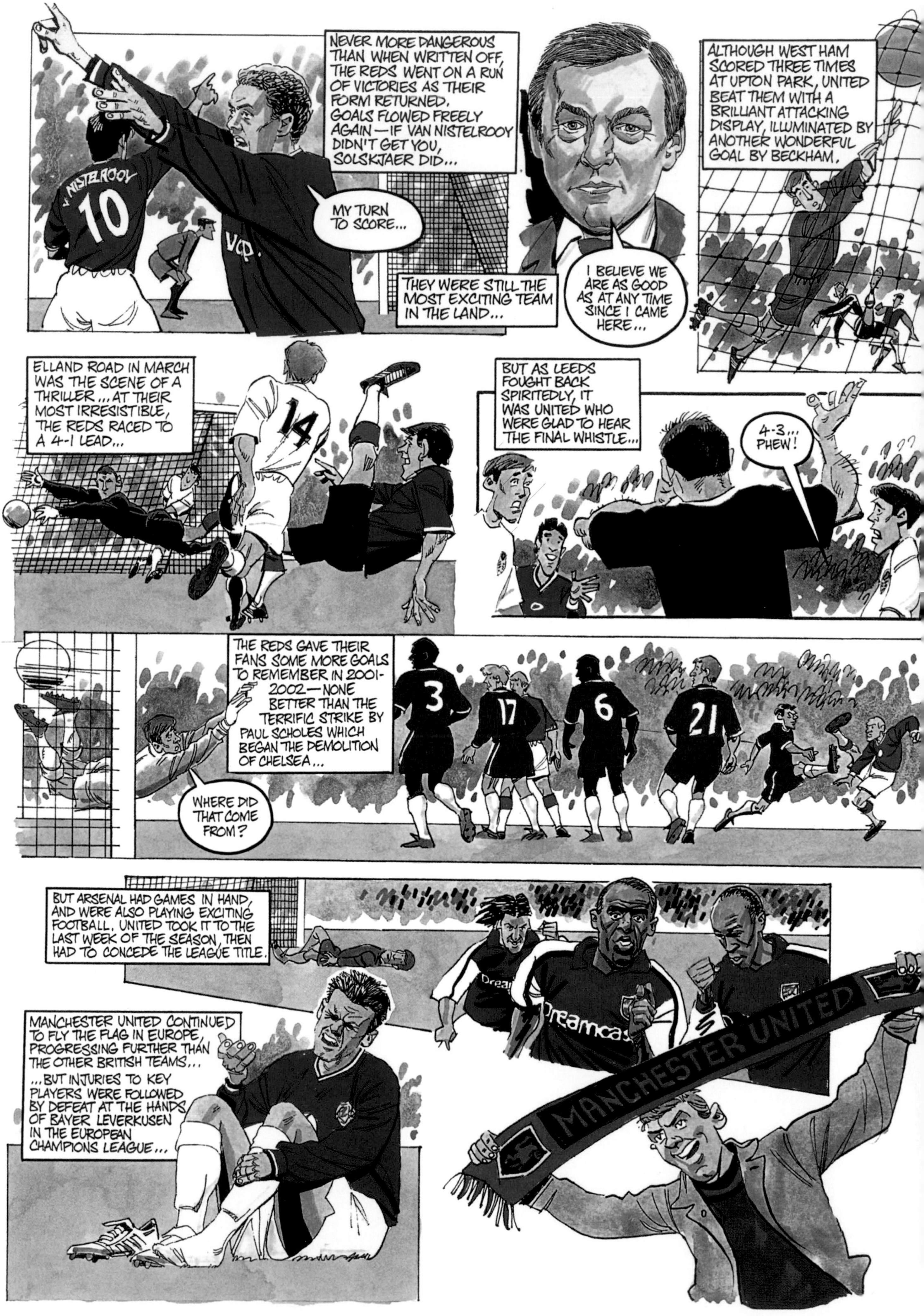
NEVER MORE DANGEROUS THAN WHEN WRITTEN OFF, THE REDS WENT ON A RUN OF VICTORIES AS THEIR FORM RETURNED. GOALS FLOWED FREELY AGAIN — IF VAN NISTELROOY DIDN'T GET YOU, SOLSKJAER DID...
NISTELROOY 10
MY TURN TO SCORE...
THEY WERE STILL THE MOST EXCITING TEAM IN THE LAND...
I BELIEVE WE ARE AS GOOD AS AT ANY TIME SINCE I CAME HERE...
ALTHOUGH WEST HAM SCORED THREE TIMES AT UPTON PARK, UNITED BEAT THEM WITH A BRILLIANT ATTACKING DISPLAY, ILLUMINATED BY ANOTHER WONDERFUL GOAL BY BECKHAM.
ELLAND ROAD IN MARCH WAS THE SCENE OF A THRILLER... AT THEIR MOST IRRESISTIBLE, THE REDS RACED TO A 4-1 LEAD...
BUT AS LEEDS FOUGHT BACK SPIRITEDLY, IT WAS UNITED WHO WERE GLAD TO HEAR THE FINAL WHISTLE...
4-3... PHEW!
THE REDS GAVE THEIR FANS SOME MORE GOALS TO REMEMBER IN 2001-2002 — NONE BETTER THAN THE TERRIFIC STRIKE BY PAUL SCHOLES WHICH BEGAN THE DEMOLITION OF CHELSEA...
WHERE DID THAT COME FROM?
BUT ARSENAL HAD GAMES IN HAND, AND WERE ALSO PLAYING EXCITING FOOTBALL. UNITED TOOK IT TO THE LAST WEEK OF THE SEASON, THEN HAD TO CONCEDE THE LEAGUE TITLE.
MANCHESTER UNITED CONTINUED TO FLY THE FLAG IN EUROPE, PROGRESSING FURTHER THAN THE OTHER BRITISH TEAMS...
...BUT INJURIES TO KEY PLAYERS WERE FOLLOWED BY DEFEAT AT THE HANDS OF BAYER LEVERKUSEN IN THE EUROPEAN CHAMPIONS LEAGUE...
MANCHESTER UNITED

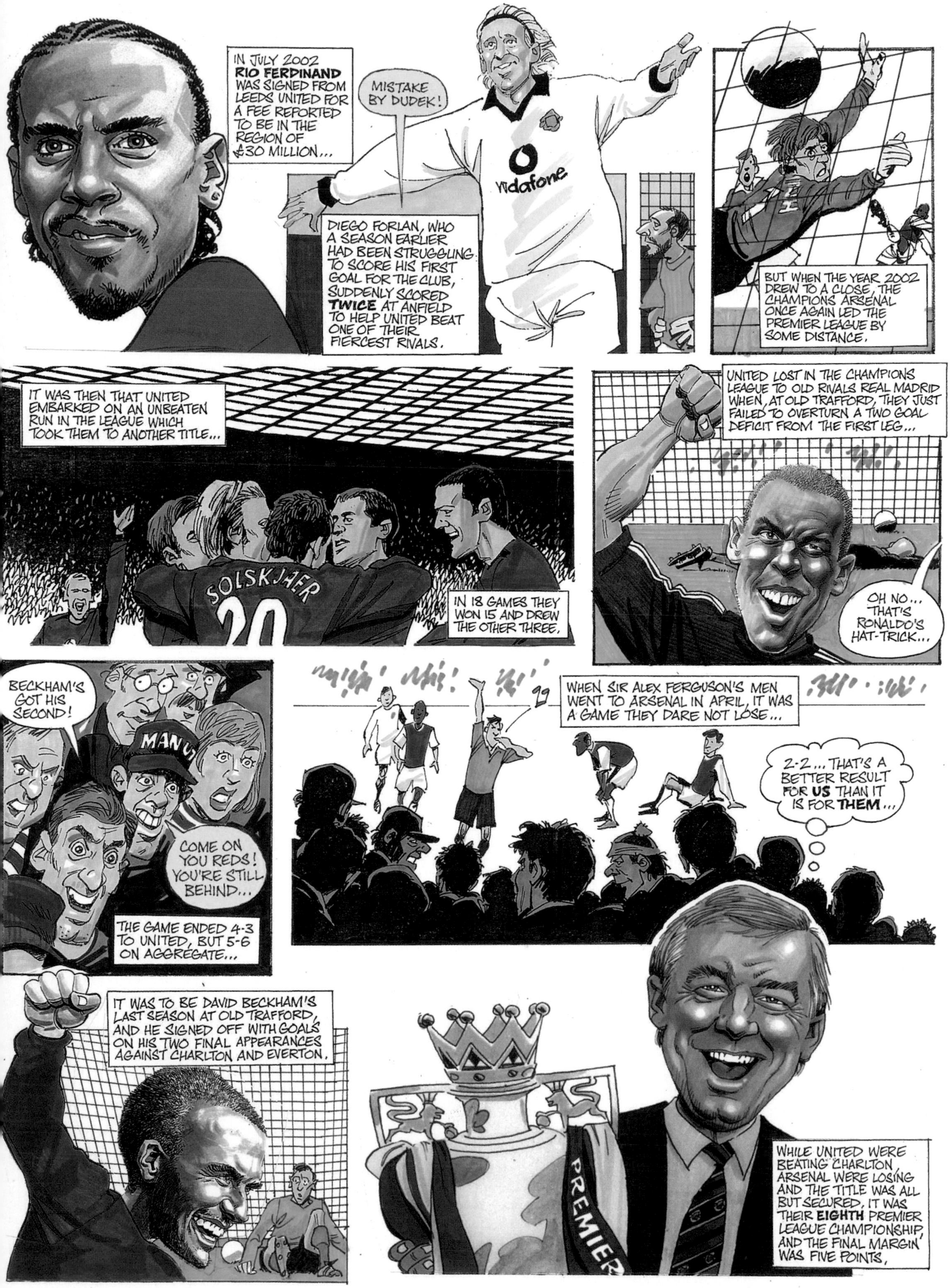
IN JULY 2002 **RIO FERDINAND** WAS SIGNED FROM LEEDS UNITED FOR A FEE REPORTED TO BE IN THE REGION OF £30 MILLION...
MISTAKE BY DUDEK!
DIEGO FORLAN, WHO A SEASON EARLIER HAD BEEN STRUGGLING TO SCORE HIS FIRST GOAL FOR THE CLUB, SUDDENLY SCORED **TWICE** AT ANFIELD TO HELP UNITED BEAT ONE OF THEIR FIERCEST RIVALS.
BUT WHEN THE YEAR 2002 DREW TO A CLOSE, THE CHAMPIONS ARSENAL ONCE AGAIN LED THE PREMIER LEAGUE BY SOME DISTANCE.
IT WAS THEN THAT UNITED EMBARKED ON AN UNBEATEN RUN IN THE LEAGUE WHICH TOOK THEM TO ANOTHER TITLE...
SOLSKJAER
20
IN 18 GAMES THEY WON 15 AND DREW THE OTHER THREE.
UNITED LOST IN THE CHAMPIONS LEAGUE TO OLD RIVALS REAL MADRID WHEN, AT OLD TRAFFORD, THEY JUST FAILED TO OVERTURN A TWO GOAL DEFICIT FROM THE FIRST LEG...
OH NO... THAT'S RONALDO'S HAT-TRICK...
BECKHAM'S GOT HIS SECOND!
MAN U
COME ON YOU REDS! YOU'RE STILL BEHIND...
THE GAME ENDED 4-3 TO UNITED, BUT 5-6 ON AGGREGATE...
WHEN SIR ALEX FERGUSON'S MEN WENT TO ARSENAL IN APRIL, IT WAS A GAME THEY DARE NOT LOSE...
2-2... THAT'S A BETTER RESULT FOR **US** THAN IT IS FOR **THEM**...
IT WAS TO BE DAVID BECKHAM'S LAST SEASON AT OLD TRAFFORD, AND HE SIGNED OFF WITH GOALS ON HIS TWO FINAL APPEARANCES AGAINST CHARLTON AND EVERTON.
PREMIER
WHILE UNITED WERE BEATING CHARLTON ARSENAL WERE LOSING AND THE TITLE WAS ALL BUT SECURED, IT WAS THEIR **EIGHTH** PREMIER LEAGUE CHAMPIONSHIP, AND THE FINAL MARGIN WAS FIVE POINTS.

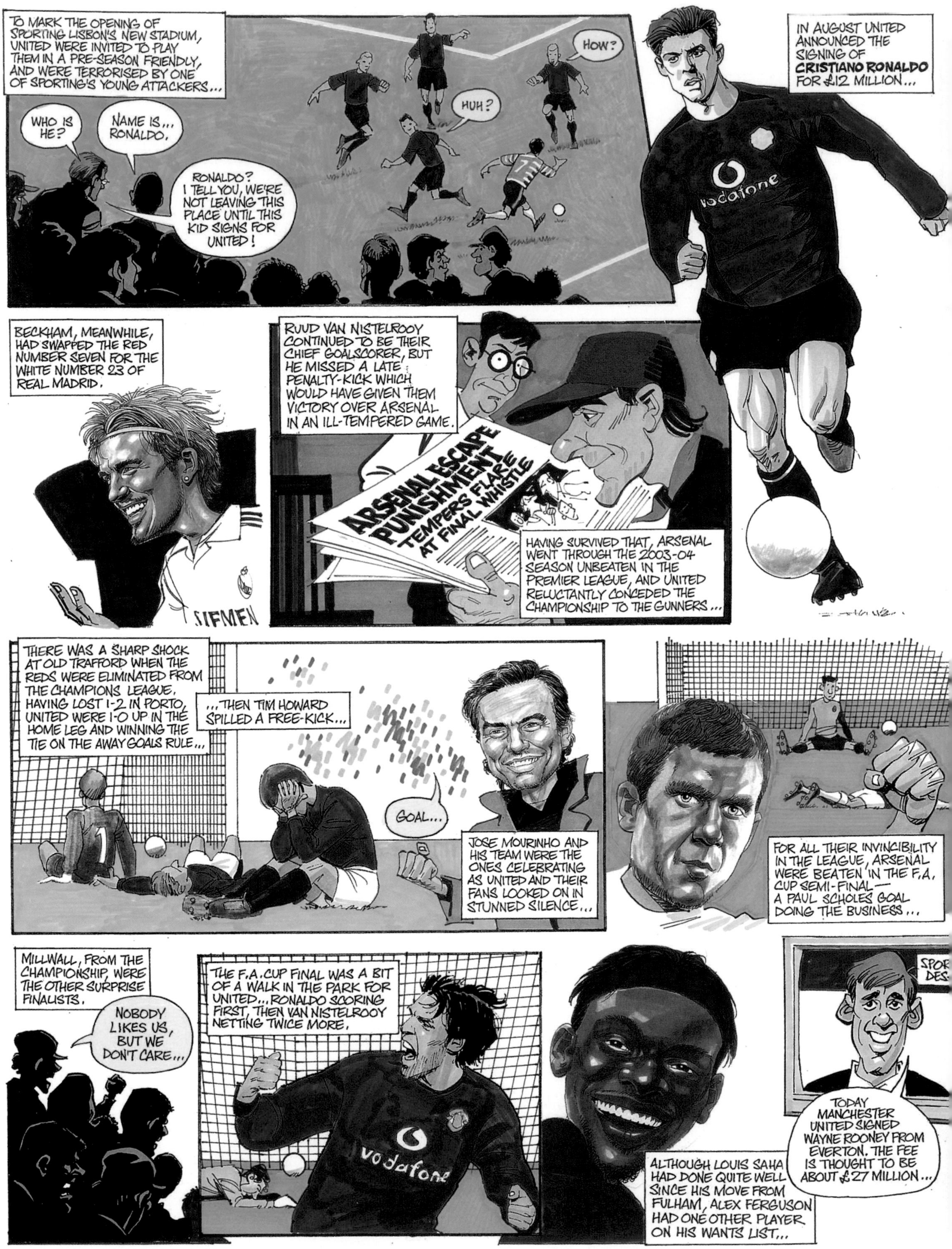
TO MARK THE OPENING OF SPORTING LISBON'S NEW STADIUM, UNITED WERE INVITED TO PLAY THEM IN A PRE-SEASON FRIENDLY, AND WERE TERRORISED BY ONE OF SPORTING'S YOUNG ATTACKERS...
WHO IS HE?
NAME IS... RONALDO.
HOW?
HUH?
RONALDO? I TELL YOU, WE'RE NOT LEAVING THIS PLACE UNTIL THIS KID SIGNS FOR UNITED!
IN AUGUST UNITED ANNOUNCED THE SIGNING OF CRISTIANO RONALDO FOR £12 MILLION...
vodafone
BECKHAM, MEANWHILE, HAD SWAPPED THE RED NUMBER SEVEN FOR THE WHITE NUMBER 23 OF REAL MADRID.
SIEMEN
RUUD VAN NISTELROOY CONTINUED TO BE THEIR CHIEF GOALSCORER, BUT HE MISSED A LATE PENALTY-KICK WHICH WOULD HAVE GIVEN THEM VICTORY OVER ARSENAL IN AN ILL-TEMPERED GAME.
ARSENAL ESCAPE PUNISHMENT
TEMPERS FLARE AT FINAL WHISTLE
HAVING SURVIVED THAT, ARSENAL WENT THROUGH THE 2003-04 SEASON UNBEATEN IN THE PREMIER LEAGUE, AND UNITED RELUCTANTLY CONCEDED THE CHAMPIONSHIP TO THE GUNNERS...
THERE WAS A SHARP SHOCK AT OLD TRAFFORD WHEN THE REDS WERE ELIMINATED FROM THE CHAMPIONS LEAGUE. HAVING LOST 1-2 IN PORTO, UNITED WERE 1-0 UP IN THE HOME LEG AND WINNING THE TIE ON THE AWAY GOALS RULE...
...THEN TIM HOWARD SPILLED A FREE-KICK...
GOAL...
JOSE MOURINHO AND HIS TEAM WERE THE ONES CELEBRATING AS UNITED AND THEIR FANS LOOKED ON IN STUNNED SILENCE...
FOR ALL THEIR INVINCIBILITY IN THE LEAGUE, ARSENAL WERE BEATEN IN THE F.A. CUP SEMI-FINAL — A PAUL SCHOLES GOAL DOING THE BUSINESS...
MILLWALL, FROM THE CHAMPIONSHIP, WERE THE OTHER SURPRISE FINALISTS.
NOBODY LIKES US, BUT WE DON'T CARE...
THE F.A. CUP FINAL WAS A BIT OF A WALK IN THE PARK FOR UNITED... RONALDO SCORING FIRST, THEN VAN NISTELROOY NETTING TWICE MORE.
vodafone
ALTHOUGH LOUIS SAHA HAD DONE QUITE WELL SINCE HIS MOVE FROM FULHAM, ALEX FERGUSON HAD ONE OTHER PLAYER ON HIS WANTS LIST...
TODAY MANCHESTER UNITED SIGNED WAYNE ROONEY FROM EVERTON. THE FEE IS THOUGHT TO BE ABOUT £27 MILLION...

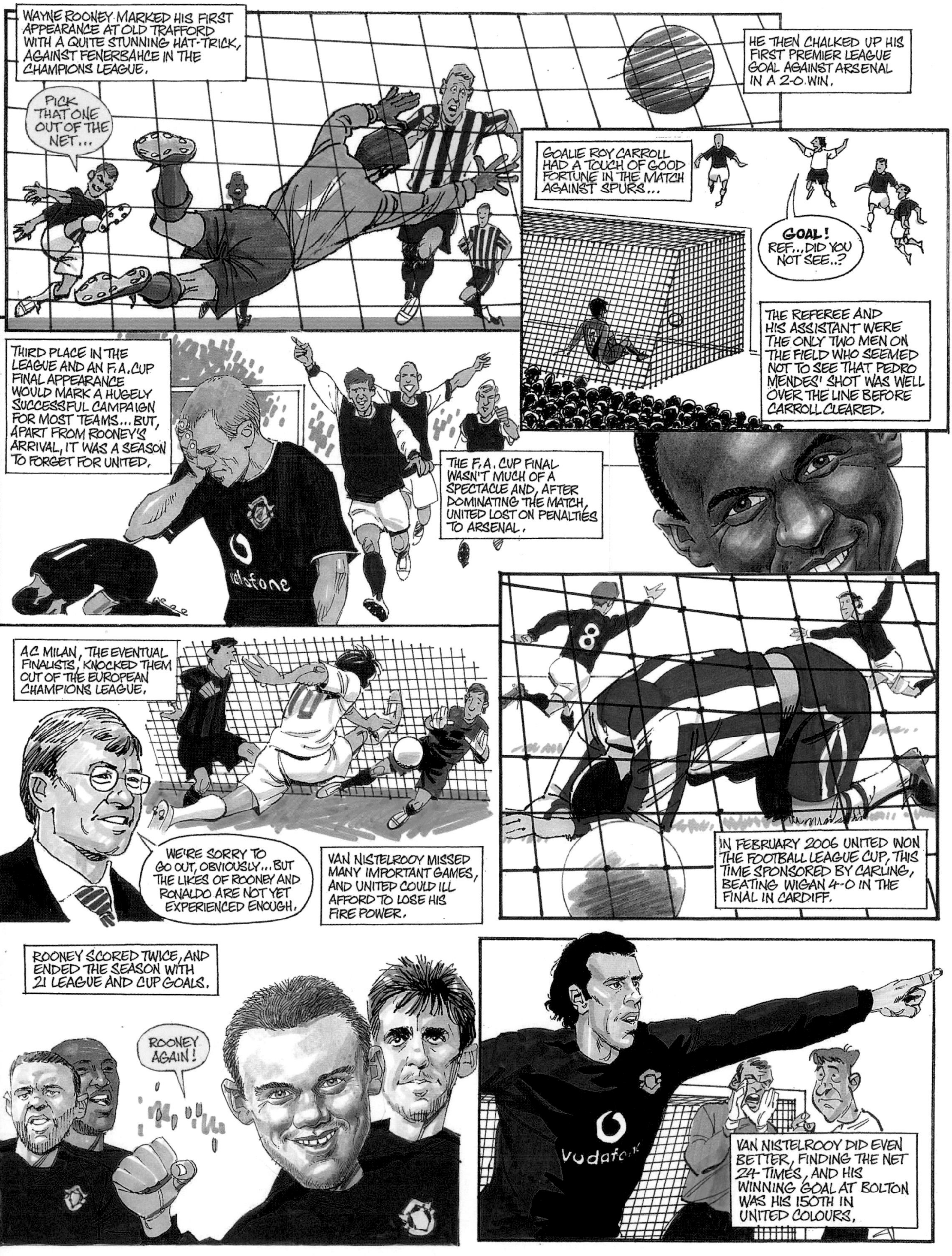
WAYNE ROONEY MARKED HIS FIRST APPEARANCE AT OLD TRAFFORD WITH A QUITE STUNNING HAT-TRICK, AGAINST FENERBAHCE IN THE CHAMPIONS LEAGUE.
PICK THAT ONE OUT OF THE NET...
HE THEN CHALKED UP HIS FIRST PREMIER LEAGUE GOAL AGAINST ARSENAL IN A 2-0 WIN.
GOALIE ROY CARROLL HAD A TOUCH OF GOOD FORTUNE IN THE MATCH AGAINST SPURS...
GOAL! REF... DID YOU NOT SEE..?
THE REFEREE AND HIS ASSISTANT WERE THE ONLY TWO MEN ON THE FIELD WHO SEEMED NOT TO SEE THAT PEDRO MENDES' SHOT WAS WELL OVER THE LINE BEFORE CARROLL CLEARED.
THIRD PLACE IN THE LEAGUE AND AN F.A. CUP FINAL APPEARANCE WOULD MARK A HUGELY SUCCESSFUL CAMPAIGN FOR MOST TEAMS... BUT, APART FROM ROONEY'S ARRIVAL, IT WAS A SEASON TO FORGET FOR UNITED.
THE F.A. CUP FINAL WASN'T MUCH OF A SPECTACLE AND, AFTER DOMINATING THE MATCH, UNITED LOST ON PENALTIES TO ARSENAL.
vodafone
AC MILAN, THE EVENTUAL FINALISTS, KNOCKED THEM OUT OF THE EUROPEAN CHAMPIONS LEAGUE.
WE'RE SORRY TO GO OUT, OBVIOUSLY... BUT THE LIKES OF ROONEY AND RONALDO ARE NOT YET EXPERIENCED ENOUGH.
VAN NISTELROOY MISSED MANY IMPORTANT GAMES, AND UNITED COULD ILL AFFORD TO LOSE HIS FIRE POWER.
IN FEBRUARY 2006 UNITED WON THE FOOTBALL LEAGUE CUP, THIS TIME SPONSORED BY CARLING, BEATING WIGAN 4-0 IN THE FINAL IN CARDIFF.
ROONEY SCORED TWICE, AND ENDED THE SEASON WITH 21 LEAGUE AND CUP GOALS.
ROONEY AGAIN!
VAN NISTELROOY DID EVEN BETTER, FINDING THE NET 24 TIMES, AND HIS WINNING GOAL AT BOLTON WAS HIS 150TH IN UNITED COLOURS.

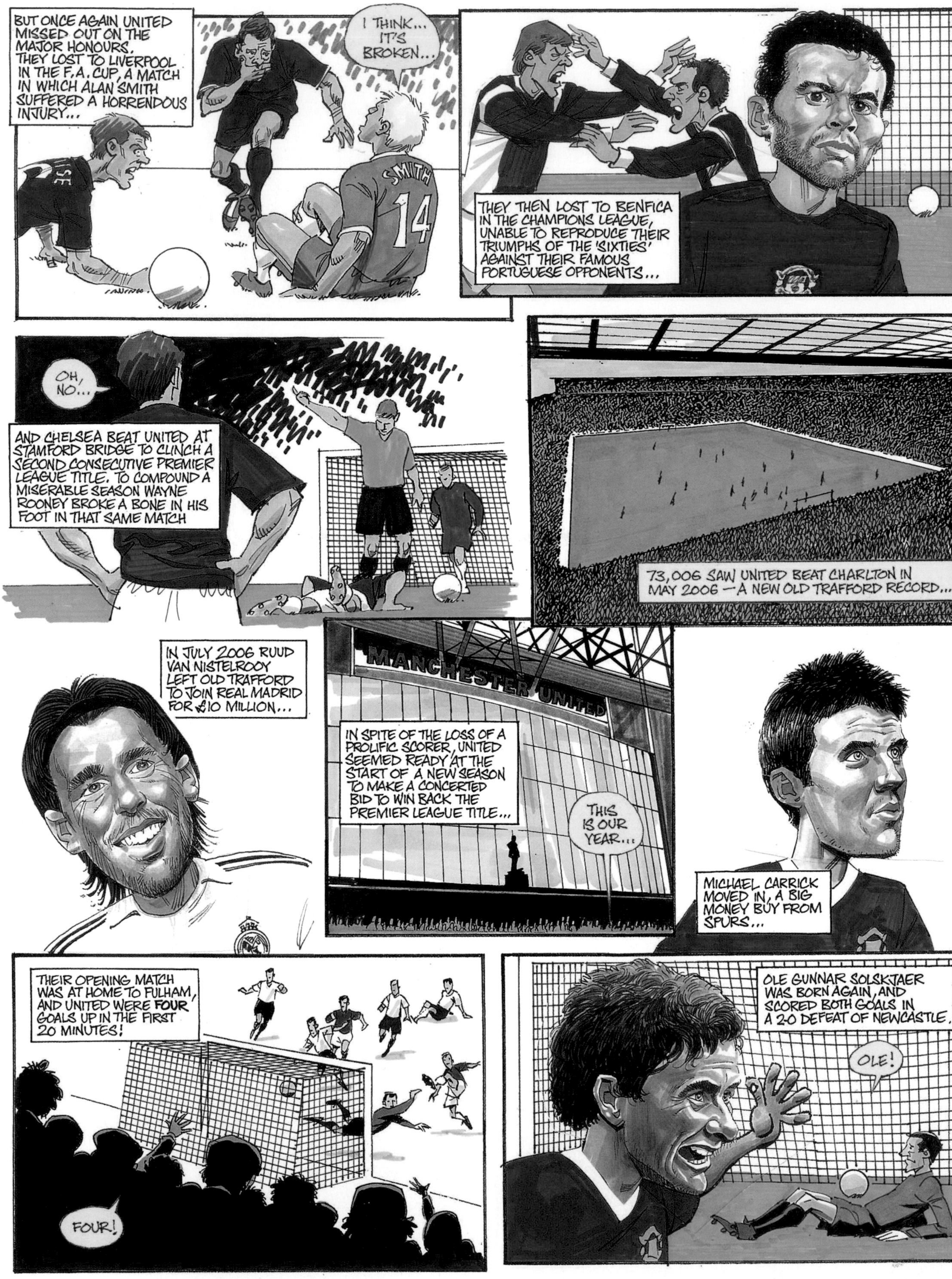
BUT ONCE AGAIN UNITED MISSED OUT ON THE MAJOR HONOURS. THEY LOST TO LIVERPOOL IN THE F.A. CUP, A MATCH IN WHICH ALAN SMITH SUFFERED A HORRENDOUS INJURY...
I THINK... IT'S BROKEN...
SMITH 14
THEY THEN LOST TO BENFICA IN THE CHAMPIONS LEAGUE, UNABLE TO REPRODUCE THEIR TRIUMPHS OF THE 'SIXTIES' AGAINST THEIR FAMOUS PORTUGUESE OPPONENTS...
OH, NO...
AND CHELSEA BEAT UNITED AT STAMFORD BRIDGE TO CLINCH A SECOND CONSECUTIVE PREMIER LEAGUE TITLE. TO COMPOUND A MISERABLE SEASON WAYNE ROONEY BROKE A BONE IN HIS FOOT IN THAT SAME MATCH
73,006 SAW UNITED BEAT CHARLTON IN MAY 2006 — A NEW OLD TRAFFORD RECORD...
IN JULY 2006 RUUD VAN NISTELROOY LEFT OLD TRAFFORD TO JOIN REAL MADRID FOR £10 MILLION...
MANCHESTER UNITED
IN SPITE OF THE LOSS OF A PROLIFIC SCORER, UNITED SEEMED READY AT THE START OF A NEW SEASON TO MAKE A CONCERTED BID TO WIN BACK THE PREMIER LEAGUE TITLE...
THIS IS OUR YEAR...
MICHAEL CARRICK MOVED IN, A BIG MONEY BUY FROM SPURS...
THEIR OPENING MATCH WAS AT HOME TO FULHAM, AND UNITED WERE FOUR GOALS UP IN THE FIRST 20 MINUTES!
FOUR!
OLE GUNNAR SOLSKJAER WAS BORN AGAIN, AND SCORED BOTH GOALS IN A 2-0 DEFEAT OF NEWCASTLE.
OLE!

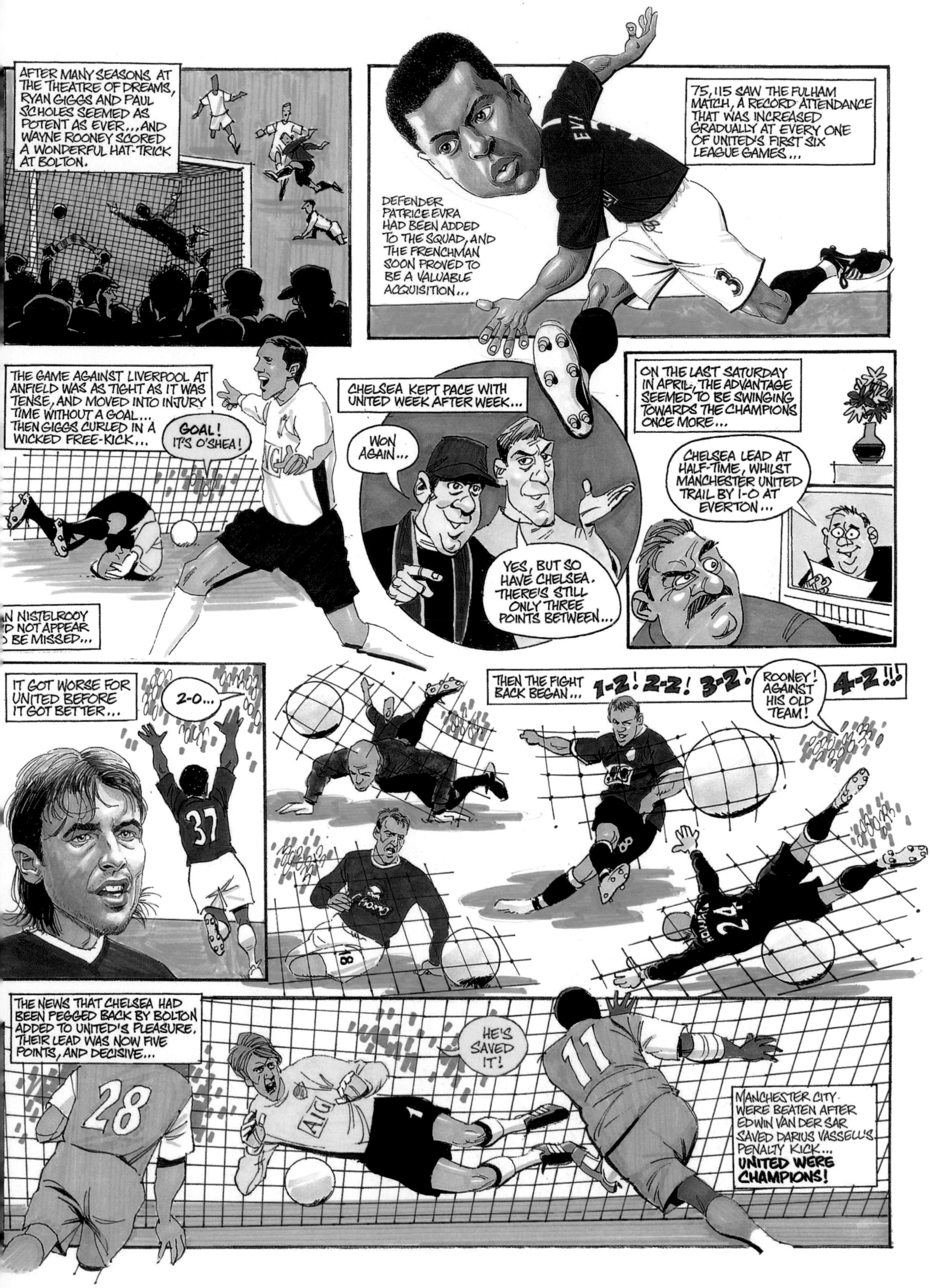
AFTER MANY SEASONS AT THE THEATRE OF DREAMS, RYAN GIGGS AND PAUL SCHOLES SEEMED AS POTENT AS EVER... AND WAYNE ROONEY SCORED A WONDERFUL HAT-TRICK AT BOLTON.
75,115 SAW THE FULHAM MATCH, A RECORD ATTENDANCE THAT WAS INCREASED GRADUALLY AT EVERY ONE OF UNITED'S FIRST SIX LEAGUE GAMES...
DEFENDER PATRICE EVRA HAD BEEN ADDED TO THE SQUAD, AND THE FRENCHMAN SOON PROVED TO BE A VALUABLE ACQUISITION...
THE GAME AGAINST LIVERPOOL AT ANFIELD WAS AS TIGHT AS IT WAS TENSE, AND MOVED INTO INJURY TIME WITHOUT A GOAL... THEN GIGGS CURLED IN A WICKED FREE-KICK...
GOAL! IT'S O'SHEA!
N NISTELROOY D NOT APPEAR BE MISSED...
CHELSEA KEPT PACE WITH UNITED WEEK AFTER WEEK...
WON AGAIN...
YES, BUT SO HAVE CHELSEA. THERE'S STILL ONLY THREE POINTS BETWEEN...
ON THE LAST SATURDAY IN APRIL, THE ADVANTAGE SEEMED TO BE SWINGING TOWARDS THE CHAMPIONS ONCE MORE...
CHELSEA LEAD AT HALF-TIME, WHILST MANCHESTER UNITED TRAIL BY 1-0 AT EVERTON...
IT GOT WORSE FOR UNITED BEFORE IT GOT BETTER...
2-0...
THEN THE FIGHT BACK BEGAN... 1-2! 2-2! 3-2!
ROONEY! AGAINST HIS OLD TEAM!
4-2!!!
THE NEWS THAT CHELSEA HAD BEEN PEGGED BACK BY BOLTON ADDED TO UNITED'S PLEASURE. THEIR LEAD WAS NOW FIVE POINTS, AND DECISIVE...
HE'S SAVED IT!
MANCHESTER CITY WERE BEATEN AFTER EDWIN VAN DER SAR SAVED DARIUS VASSELL'S PENALTY KICK... UNITED WERE CHAMPIONS!

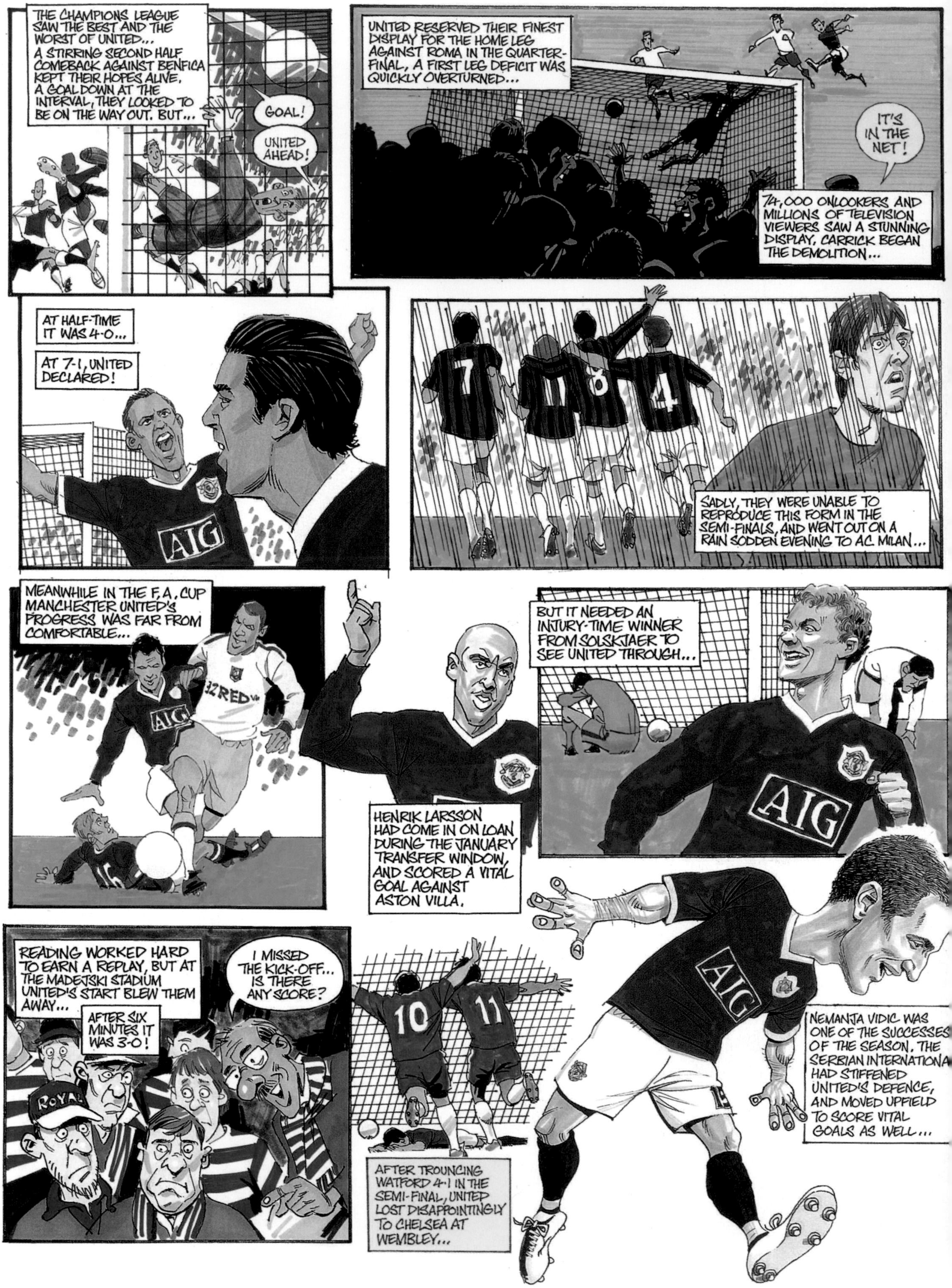
THE CHAMPIONS LEAGUE SAW THE BEST AND THE WORST OF UNITED... A STIRRING SECOND HALF COMEBACK AGAINST BENFICA KEPT THEIR HOPES ALIVE. A GOAL DOWN AT THE INTERVAL, THEY LOOKED TO BE ON THE WAY OUT. BUT...
GOAL!
UNITED AHEAD!
UNITED RESERVED THEIR FINEST DISPLAY FOR THE HOME LEG AGAINST ROMA IN THE QUARTER-FINAL, A FIRST LEG DEFICIT WAS QUICKLY OVERTURNED...
IT'S IN THE NET!
74,000 ONLOOKERS AND MILLIONS OF TELEVISION VIEWERS SAW A STUNNING DISPLAY. CARRICK BEGAN THE DEMOLITION...
AT HALF-TIME IT WAS 4-0...
AT 7-1, UNITED DECLARED!
AIG
SADLY, THEY WERE UNABLE TO REPRODUCE THIS FORM IN THE SEMI-FINALS, AND WENT OUT ON A RAIN SODDEN EVENING TO AC MILAN...
MEANWHILE IN THE F.A. CUP MANCHESTER UNITED'S PROGRESS WAS FAR FROM COMFORTABLE...
32RED
AIG
HENRIK LARSSON HAD COME IN ON LOAN DURING THE JANUARY TRANSFER WINDOW, AND SCORED A VITAL GOAL AGAINST ASTON VILLA.
BUT IT NEEDED AN INJURY-TIME WINNER FROM SOLSKJAER TO SEE UNITED THROUGH...
AIG
READING WORKED HARD TO EARN A REPLAY, BUT AT THE MADEJSKI STADIUM UNITED'S START BLEW THEM AWAY...
AFTER SIX MINUTES IT WAS 3-0!
I MISSED THE KICK-OFF... IS THERE ANY SCORE?
ROYAL
AFTER TROUNCING WATFORD 4-1 IN THE SEMI-FINAL, UNITED LOST DISAPPOINTINGLY TO CHELSEA AT WEMBLEY...
AIG
NEMANJA VIDIC WAS ONE OF THE SUCCESSES OF THE SEASON. THE SERBIAN INTERNATIONA HAD STIFFENED UNITED'S DEFENCE, AND MOVED UPFIELD TO SCORE VITAL GOALS AS WELL...

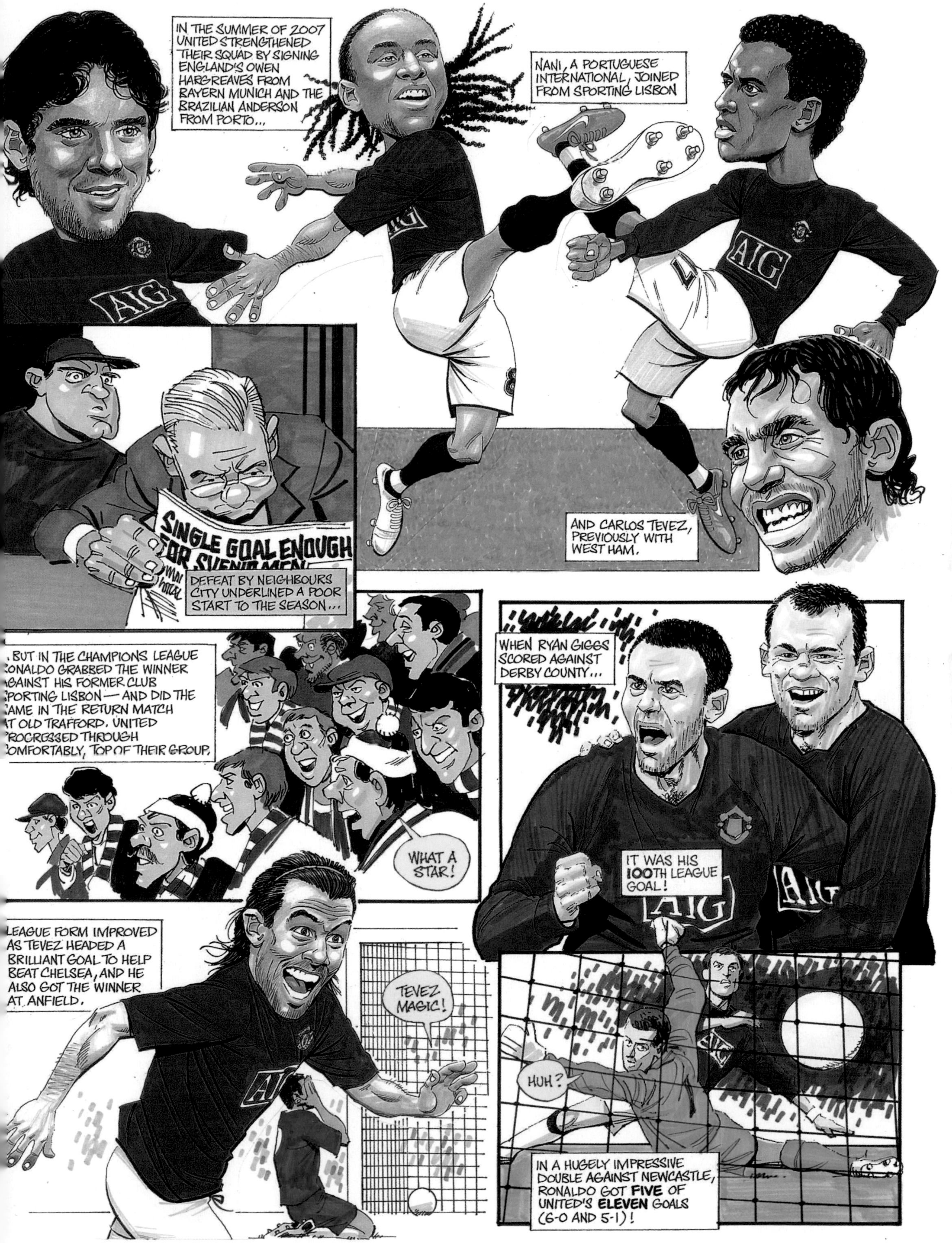

IN THE SUMMER OF 2007 UNITED STRENGTHENED THEIR SQUAD BY SIGNING ENGLAND'S OWEN HARGREAVES FROM BAYERN MUNICH AND THE BRAZILIAN ANDERSON FROM PORTO...
NANI, A PORTUGUESE INTERNATIONAL, JOINED FROM SPORTING LISBON
AND CARLOS TEVEZ, PREVIOUSLY WITH WEST HAM.
SINGLE GOAL ENOUGH
DEFEAT BY NEIGHBOURS CITY UNDERLINED A POOR START TO THE SEASON...
...BUT IN THE CHAMPIONS LEAGUE RONALDO GRABBED THE WINNER AGAINST HIS FORMER CLUB SPORTING LISBON — AND DID THE SAME IN THE RETURN MATCH AT OLD TRAFFORD. UNITED PROGRESSED THROUGH COMFORTABLY, TOP OF THEIR GROUP.
WHAT A STAR!
WHEN RYAN GIGGS SCORED AGAINST DERBY COUNTY...
IT WAS HIS 100TH LEAGUE GOAL!
LEAGUE FORM IMPROVED AS TEVEZ HEADED A BRILLIANT GOAL TO HELP BEAT CHELSEA, AND HE ALSO GOT THE WINNER AT ANFIELD.
TEVEZ MAGIC!
HUH?
IN A HUGELY IMPRESSIVE DOUBLE AGAINST NEWCASTLE, RONALDO GOT FIVE OF UNITED'S ELEVEN GOALS (6-0 AND 5-1)!

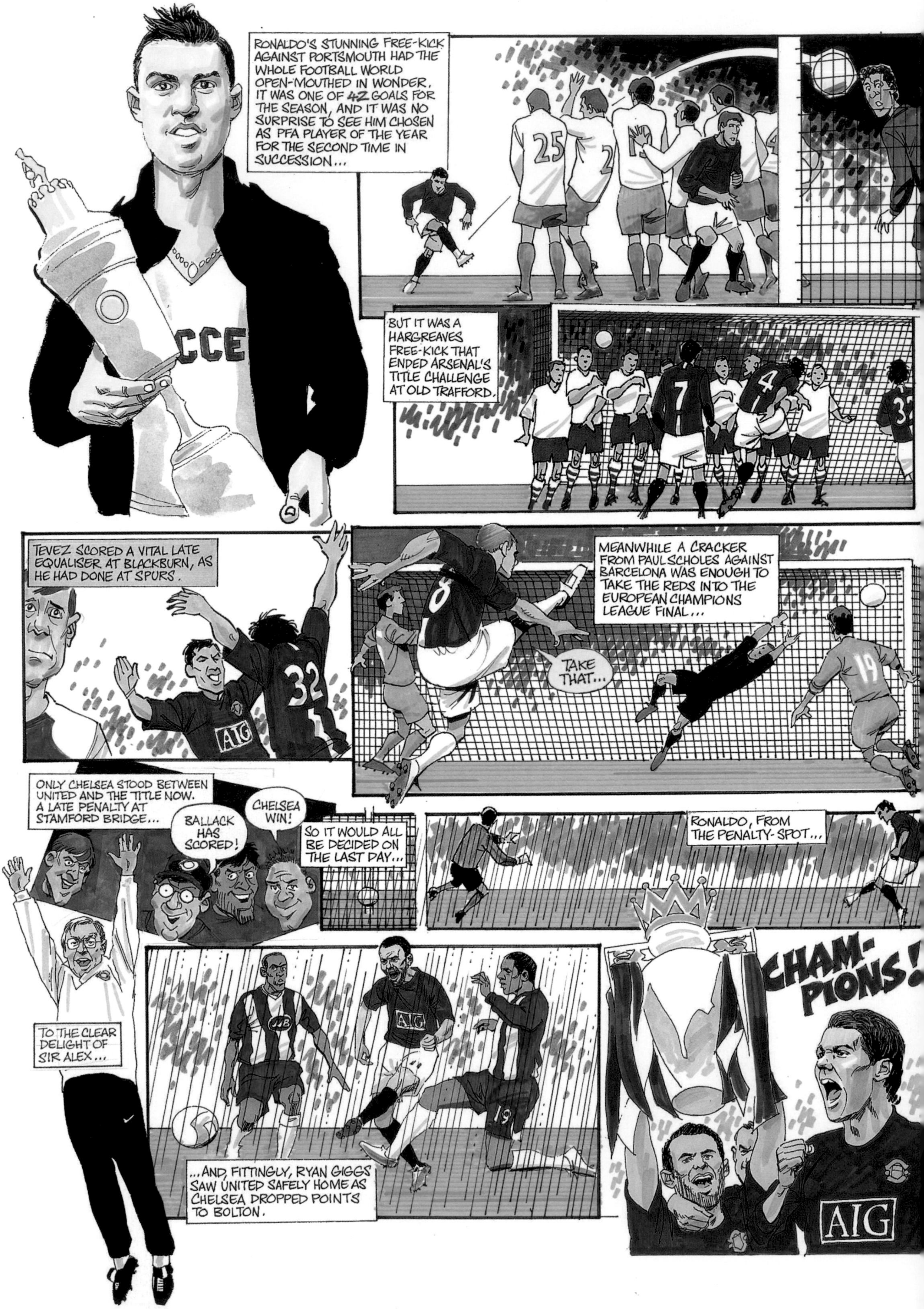
RONALDO'S STUNNING FREE-KICK AGAINST PORTSMOUTH HAD THE WHOLE FOOTBALL WORLD OPEN-MOUTHED IN WONDER. IT WAS ONE OF 42 GOALS FOR THE SEASON, AND IT WAS NO SURPRISE TO SEE HIM CHOSEN AS PFA PLAYER OF THE YEAR FOR THE SECOND TIME IN SUCCESSION...
BUT IT WAS A HARGREAVES FREE-KICK THAT ENDED ARSENAL'S TITLE CHALLENGE AT OLD TRAFFORD.
TEVEZ SCORED A VITAL LATE EQUALISER AT BLACKBURN, AS HE HAD DONE AT SPURS.
MEANWHILE A CRACKER FROM PAUL SCHOLES AGAINST BARCELONA WAS ENOUGH TO TAKE THE REDS INTO THE EUROPEAN CHAMPIONS LEAGUE FINAL...
TAKE THAT...
ONLY CHELSEA STOOD BETWEEN UNITED AND THE TITLE NOW. A LATE PENALTY AT STAMFORD BRIDGE...
BALLACK HAS SCORED!
CHELSEA WIN!
SO IT WOULD ALL BE DECIDED ON THE LAST DAY...
RONALDO, FROM THE PENALTY-SPOT...
TO THE CLEAR DELIGHT OF SIR ALEX...
...AND, FITTINGLY, RYAN GIGGS SAW UNITED SAFELY HOME AS CHELSEA DROPPED POINTS TO BOLTON.
CHAMPIONS!

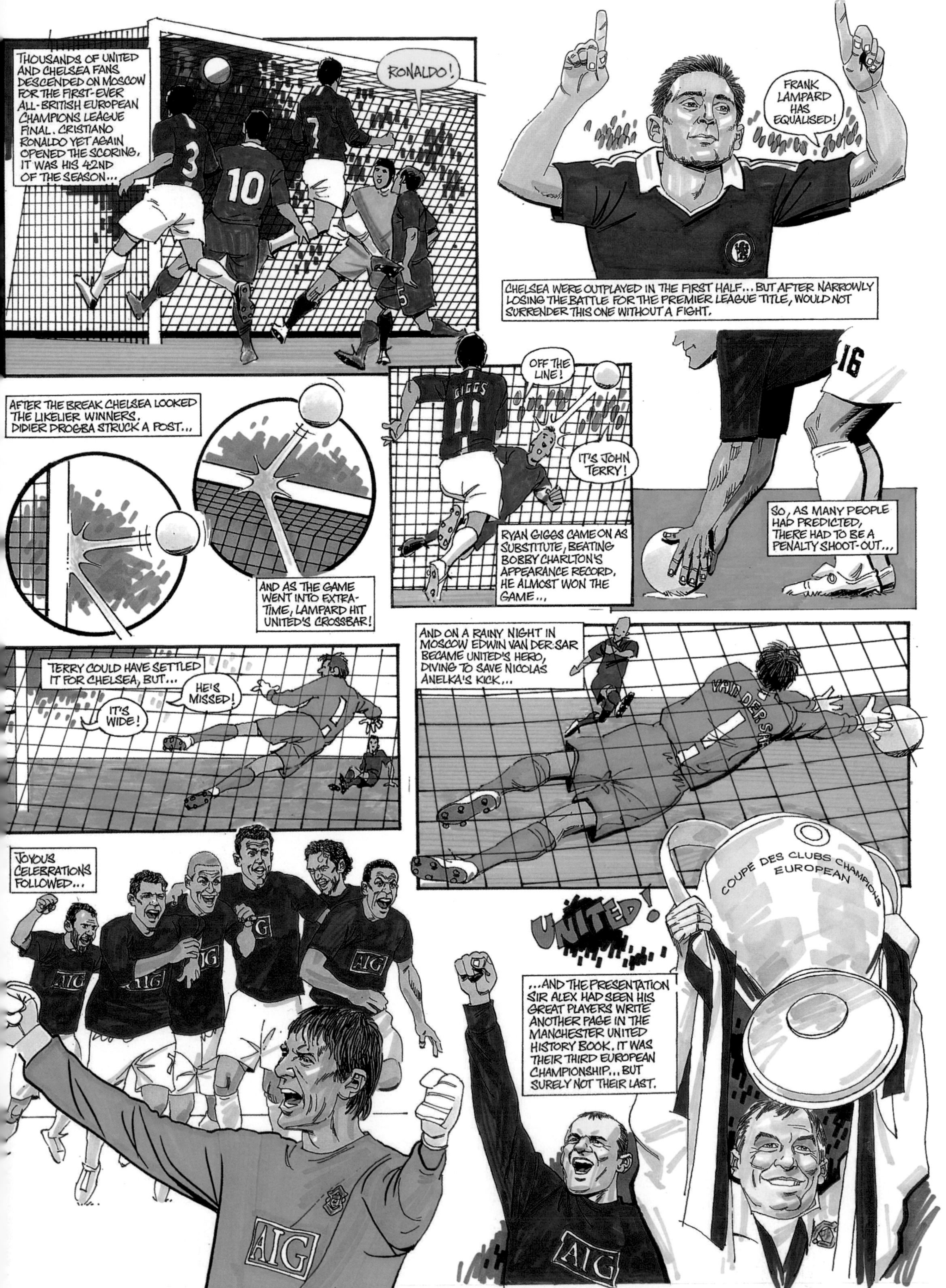
THOUSANDS OF UNITED AND CHELSEA FANS DESCENDED ON MOSCOW FOR THE FIRST-EVER ALL-BRITISH EUROPEAN CHAMPIONS LEAGUE FINAL. CRISTIANO RONALDO YET AGAIN OPENED THE SCORING, IT WAS HIS 42ND OF THE SEASON...
RONALDO!
FRANK LAMPARD HAS EQUALISED!
CHELSEA WERE OUTPLAYED IN THE FIRST HALF... BUT AFTER NARROWLY LOSING THE BATTLE FOR THE PREMIER LEAGUE TITLE, WOULD NOT SURRENDER THIS ONE WITHOUT A FIGHT.
AFTER THE BREAK CHELSEA LOOKED THE LIKELIER WINNERS. DIDIER DROGBA STRUCK A POST...
AND AS THE GAME WENT INTO EXTRA-TIME, LAMPARD HIT UNITED'S CROSSBAR!
OFF THE LINE!
IT'S JOHN TERRY!
RYAN GIGGS CAME ON AS SUBSTITUTE, BEATING BOBBY CHARLTON'S APPEARANCE RECORD. HE ALMOST WON THE GAME...
SO, AS MANY PEOPLE HAD PREDICTED, THERE HAD TO BE A PENALTY SHOOT-OUT...
TERRY COULD HAVE SETTLED IT FOR CHELSEA, BUT...
HE'S MISSED!
IT'S WIDE!
AND ON A RAINY NIGHT IN MOSCOW EDWIN VAN DER SAR BECAME UNITED'S HERO, DIVING TO SAVE NICOLAS ANELKA'S KICK...
JOYOUS CELEBRATIONS FOLLOWED...
UNITED!
COUPE DES CLUBS CHAMPIONS EUROPEAN
...AND THE PRESENTATION SIR ALEX HAD SEEN HIS GREAT PLAYERS WRITE ANOTHER PAGE IN THE MANCHESTER UNITED HISTORY BOOK. IT WAS THEIR THIRD EUROPEAN CHAMPIONSHIP... BUT SURELY NOT THEIR LAST.

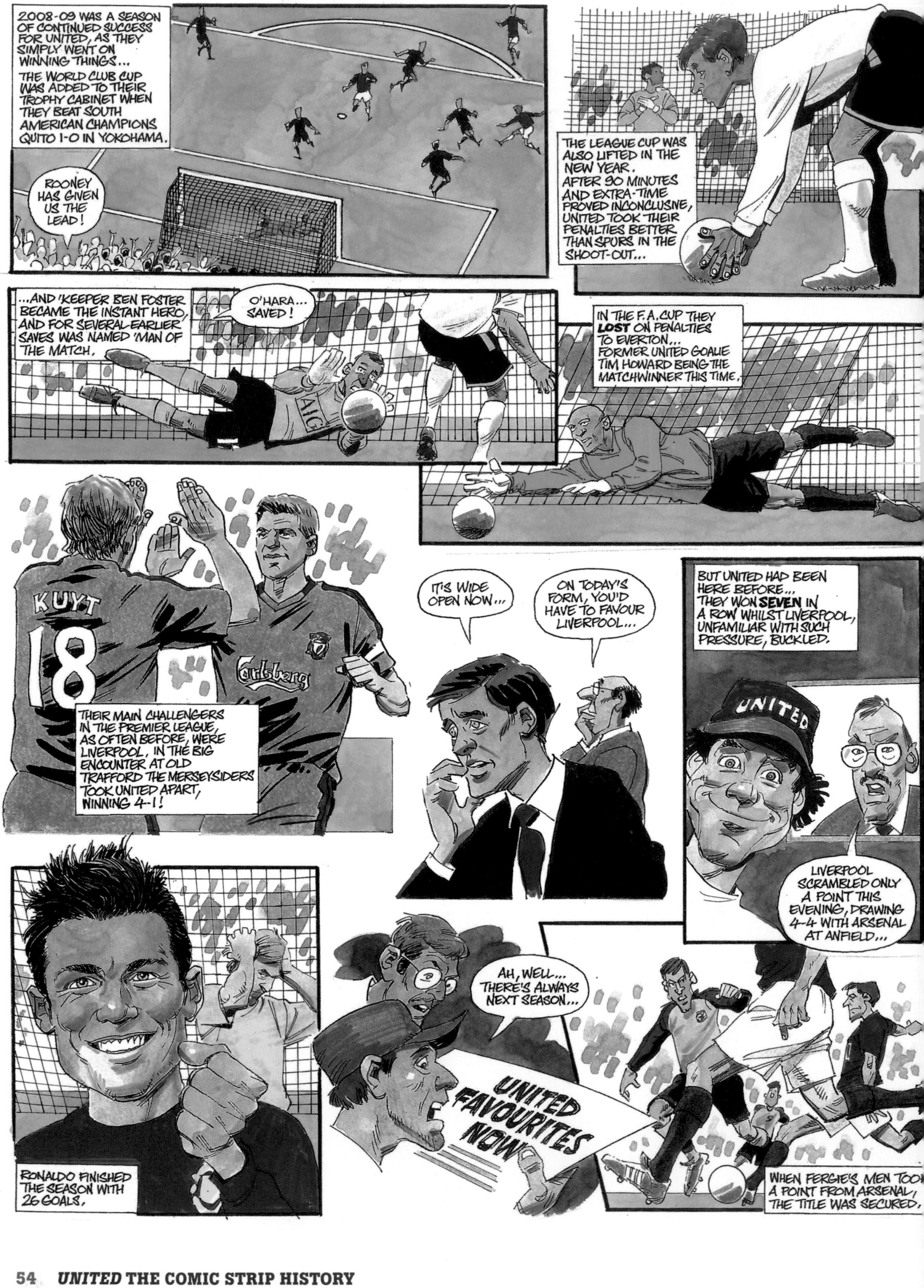

2008-09 WAS A SEASON OF CONTINUED SUCCESS FOR UNITED, AS THEY SIMPLY WENT ON WINNING THINGS...
THE WORLD CLUB CUP WAS ADDED TO THEIR TROPHY CABINET WHEN THEY BEAT SOUTH AMERICAN CHAMPIONS QUITO 1-0 IN YOKOHAMA.
ROONEY HAS GIVEN US THE LEAD!
THE LEAGUE CUP WAS ALSO LIFTED IN THE NEW YEAR. AFTER 90 MINUTES AND EXTRA-TIME PROVED INCONCLUSIVE, UNITED TOOK THEIR PENALTIES BETTER THAN SPURS IN THE SHOOT-OUT...
...AND 'KEEPER BEN FOSTER BECAME THE INSTANT HERO, AND FOR SEVERAL EARLIER SAVES WAS NAMED 'MAN OF THE MATCH.
O'HARA... SAVED!
AIG
IN THE F.A. CUP THEY **LOST** ON PENALTIES TO EVERTON... FORMER UNITED GOALIE TIM HOWARD BEING THE MATCHWINNER THIS TIME.
KUYT
18
Carlsberg
THEIR MAIN CHALLENGERS IN THE PREMIER LEAGUE, AS OFTEN BEFORE, WERE LIVERPOOL. IN THE BIG ENCOUNTER AT OLD TRAFFORD THE MERSEYSIDERS TOOK UNITED APART, WINNING 4-1!
IT'S WIDE OPEN NOW...
ON TODAY'S FORM, YOU'D HAVE TO FAVOUR LIVERPOOL...
BUT UNITED HAD BEEN HERE BEFORE... THEY WON **SEVEN** IN A ROW WHILST LIVERPOOL, UNFAMILIAR WITH SUCH PRESSURE, BUCKLED.
UNITED
LIVERPOOL SCRAMBLED ONLY A POINT THIS EVENING, DRAWING 4-4 WITH ARSENAL AT ANFIELD...
AH, WELL... THERE'S ALWAYS NEXT SEASON...
UNITED FAVOURITES NOW
RONALDO FINISHED THE SEASON WITH 26 GOALS.
WHEN FERGIE'S MEN TOOK A POINT FROM ARSENAL, THE TITLE WAS SECURED.

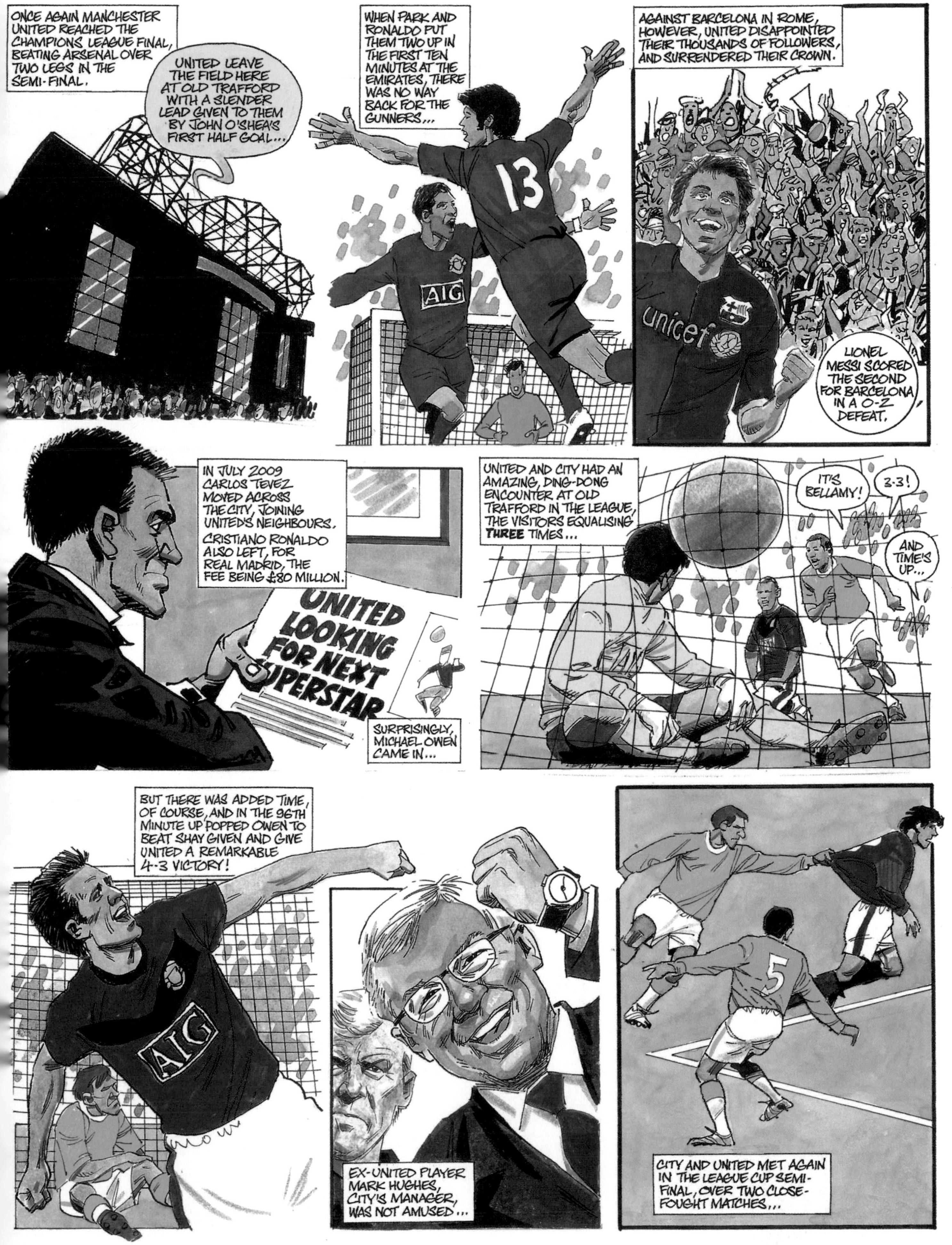

ONCE AGAIN MANCHESTER UNITED REACHED THE CHAMPIONS LEAGUE FINAL, BEATING ARSENAL OVER TWO LEGS IN THE SEMI-FINAL.
UNITED LEAVE THE FIELD HERE AT OLD TRAFFORD WITH A SLENDER LEAD GIVEN TO THEM BY JOHN O'SHEA'S FIRST HALF GOAL...
WHEN PARK AND RONALDO PUT THEM TWO UP IN THE FIRST TEN MINUTES AT THE EMIRATES, THERE WAS NO WAY BACK FOR THE GUNNERS...
13
AIG
AGAINST BARCELONA IN ROME, HOWEVER, UNITED DISAPPOINTED THEIR THOUSANDS OF FOLLOWERS, AND SURRENDERED THEIR CROWN.
unicef
LIONEL MESSI SCORED THE SECOND FOR BARCELONA IN A 0-2 DEFEAT.
IN JULY 2009 CARLOS TEVEZ MOVED ACROSS THE CITY, JOINING UNITED'S NEIGHBOURS.
CRISTIANO RONALDO ALSO LEFT, FOR REAL MADRID, THE FEE BEING £80 MILLION.
UNITED LOOKING FOR NEXT SUPERSTAR
SURPRISINGLY, MICHAEL OWEN CAME IN...
UNITED AND CITY HAD AN AMAZING, DING-DONG ENCOUNTER AT OLD TRAFFORD IN THE LEAGUE, THE VISITORS EQUALISING **THREE** TIMES...
IT'S BELLAMY!
3-3!
AND TIME'S UP...
BUT THERE WAS ADDED TIME, OF COURSE, AND IN THE 96TH MINUTE UP POPPED OWEN TO BEAT SHAY GIVEN AND GIVE UNITED A REMARKABLE 4-3 VICTORY!
AIG
EX-UNITED PLAYER MARK HUGHES, CITY'S MANAGER, WAS NOT AMUSED...
5
CITY AND UNITED MET AGAIN IN THE LEAGUE CUP SEMI-FINAL, OVER TWO CLOSE-FOUGHT MATCHES...

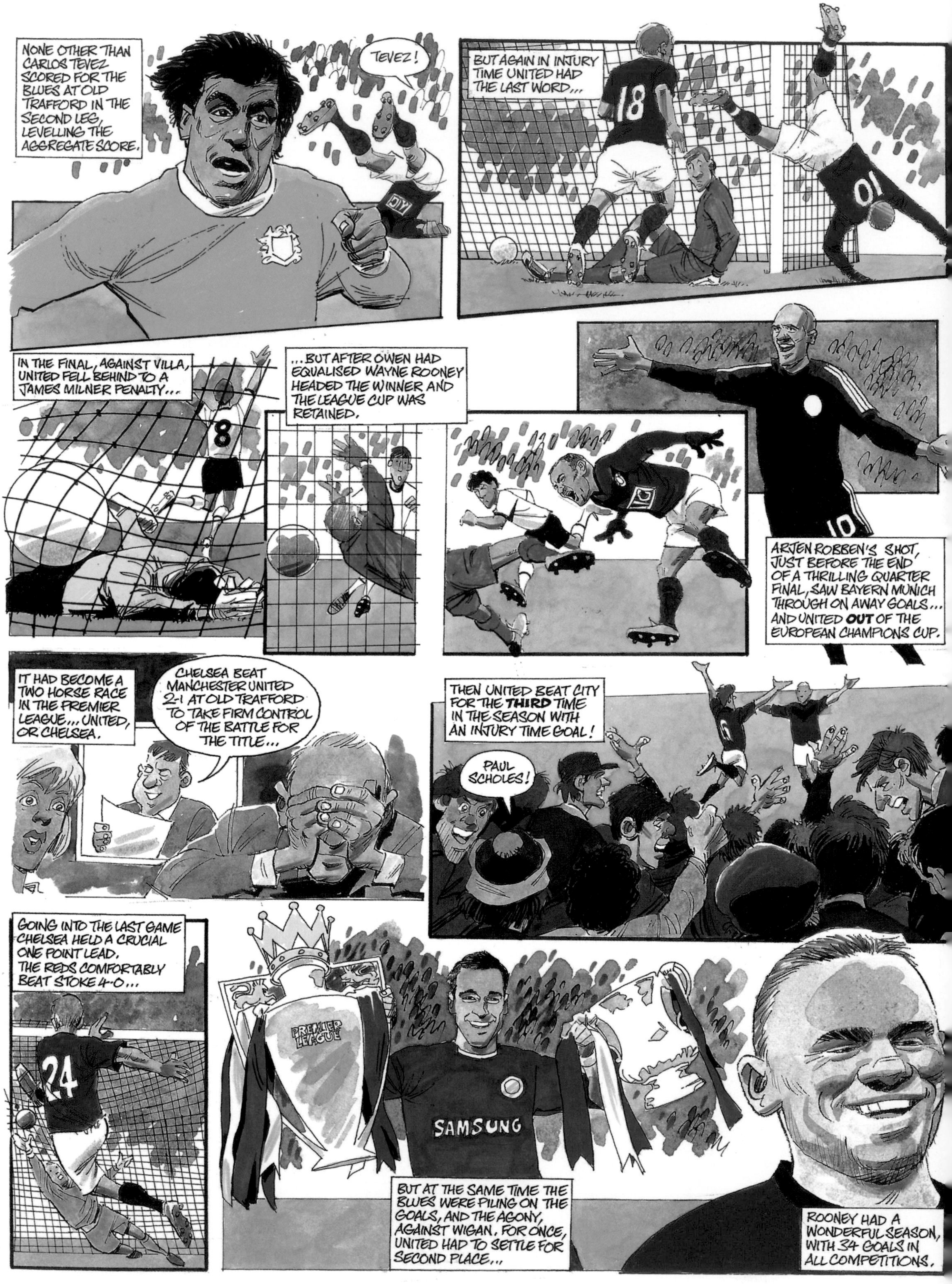
NONE OTHER THAN CARLOS TEVEZ SCORED FOR THE BLUES AT OLD TRAFFORD IN THE SECOND LEG, LEVELLING THE AGGREGATE SCORE.
TEVEZ!
BUT AGAIN IN INJURY TIME UNITED HAD THE LAST WORD...
18
10
IN THE FINAL, AGAINST VILLA, UNITED FELL BEHIND TO A JAMES MILNER PENALTY...
8
...BUT AFTER OWEN HAD EQUALISED WAYNE ROONEY HEADED THE WINNER AND THE LEAGUE CUP WAS RETAINED.
10
ARJEN ROBBEN'S SHOT, JUST BEFORE THE END OF A THRILLING QUARTER FINAL, SAW BAYERN MUNICH THROUGH ON AWAY GOALS... AND UNITED OUT OF THE EUROPEAN CHAMPIONS CUP.
IT HAD BECOME A TWO HORSE RACE IN THE PREMIER LEAGUE... UNITED, OR CHELSEA.
CHELSEA BEAT MANCHESTER UNITED 2-1 AT OLD TRAFFORD TO TAKE FIRM CONTROL OF THE BATTLE FOR THE TITLE...
THEN UNITED BEAT CITY FOR THE THIRD TIME IN THE SEASON WITH AN INJURY TIME GOAL!
PAUL SCHOLES!
GOING INTO THE LAST GAME CHELSEA HELD A CRUCIAL ONE POINT LEAD. THE REDS COMFORTABLY BEAT STOKE 4-0...
24
PREMIER LEAGUE
SAMSUNG
BUT AT THE SAME TIME THE BLUES WERE PILING ON THE GOALS, AND THE AGONY, AGAINST WIGAN. FOR ONCE, UNITED HAD TO SETTLE FOR SECOND PLACE...
ROONEY HAD A WONDERFUL SEASON, WITH 34 GOALS IN ALL COMPETITIONS.

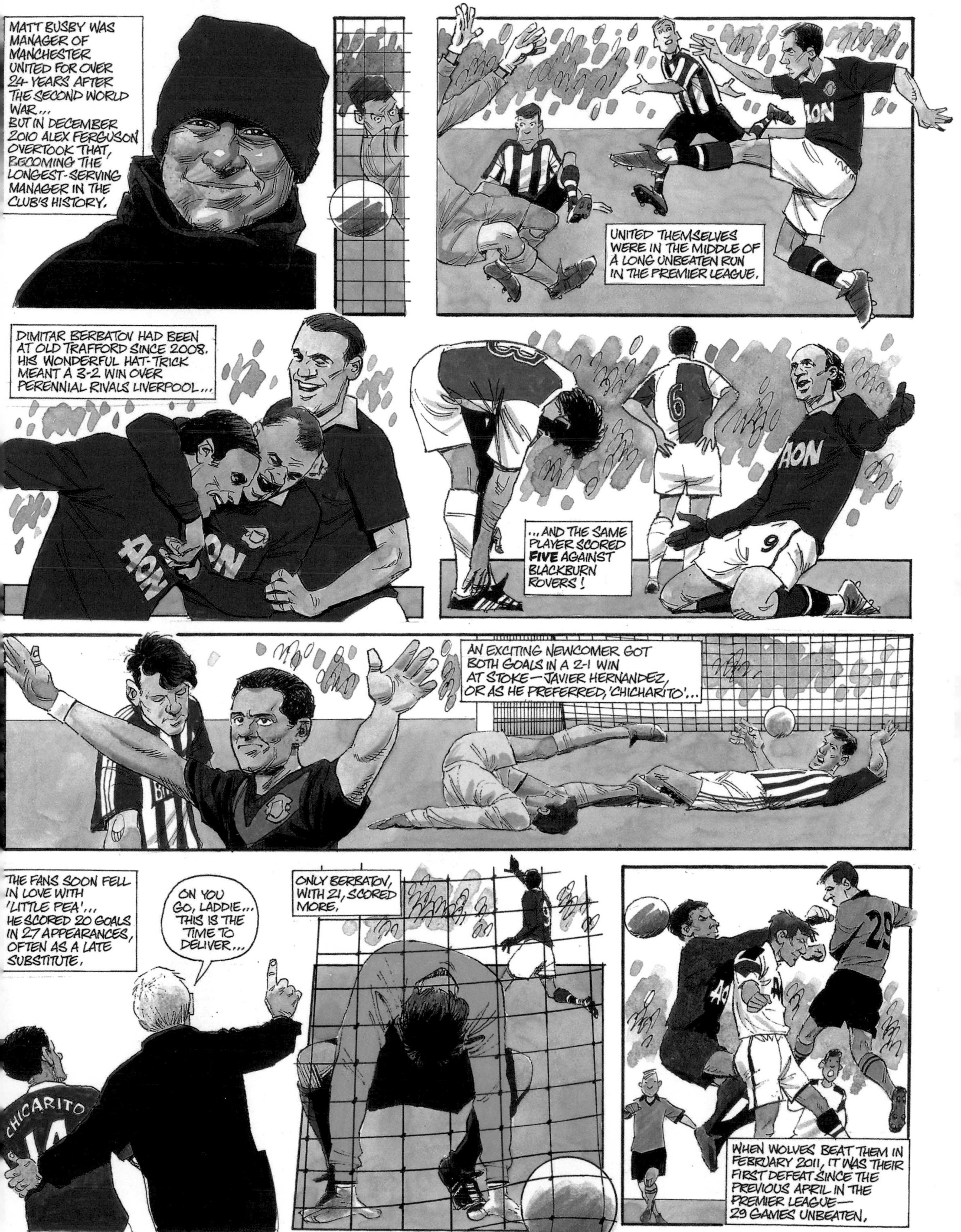
MATT BUSBY WAS MANAGER OF MANCHESTER UNITED FOR OVER 24 YEARS AFTER THE SECOND WORLD WAR... BUT IN DECEMBER 2010 ALEX FERGUSON OVERTOOK THAT, BECOMING THE LONGEST-SERVING MANAGER IN THE CLUB'S HISTORY.
UNITED THEMSELVES WERE IN THE MIDDLE OF A LONG UNBEATEN RUN IN THE PREMIER LEAGUE.
DIMITAR BERBATOV HAD BEEN AT OLD TRAFFORD SINCE 2008. HIS WONDERFUL HAT-TRICK MEANT A 3-2 WIN OVER PERENNIAL RIVALS LIVERPOOL...
AON
...AND THE SAME PLAYER SCORED **FIVE** AGAINST BLACKBURN ROVERS!
AN EXCITING NEWCOMER GOT BOTH GOALS IN A 2-1 WIN AT STOKE — JAVIER HERNANDEZ, OR AS HE PREFERRED, 'CHICHARITO'...
THE FANS SOON FELL IN LOVE WITH 'LITTLE PEA'... HE SCORED 20 GOALS IN 27 APPEARANCES, OFTEN AS A LATE SUBSTITUTE.
ON YOU GO, LADDIE... THIS IS THE TIME TO DELIVER...
CHICARITO
14
ONLY BERBATOV, WITH 21, SCORED MORE.
29
WHEN WOLVES BEAT THEM IN FEBRUARY 2011, IT WAS THEIR FIRST DEFEAT SINCE THE PREVIOUS APRIL IN THE PREMIER LEAGUE — 29 GAMES UNBEATEN.

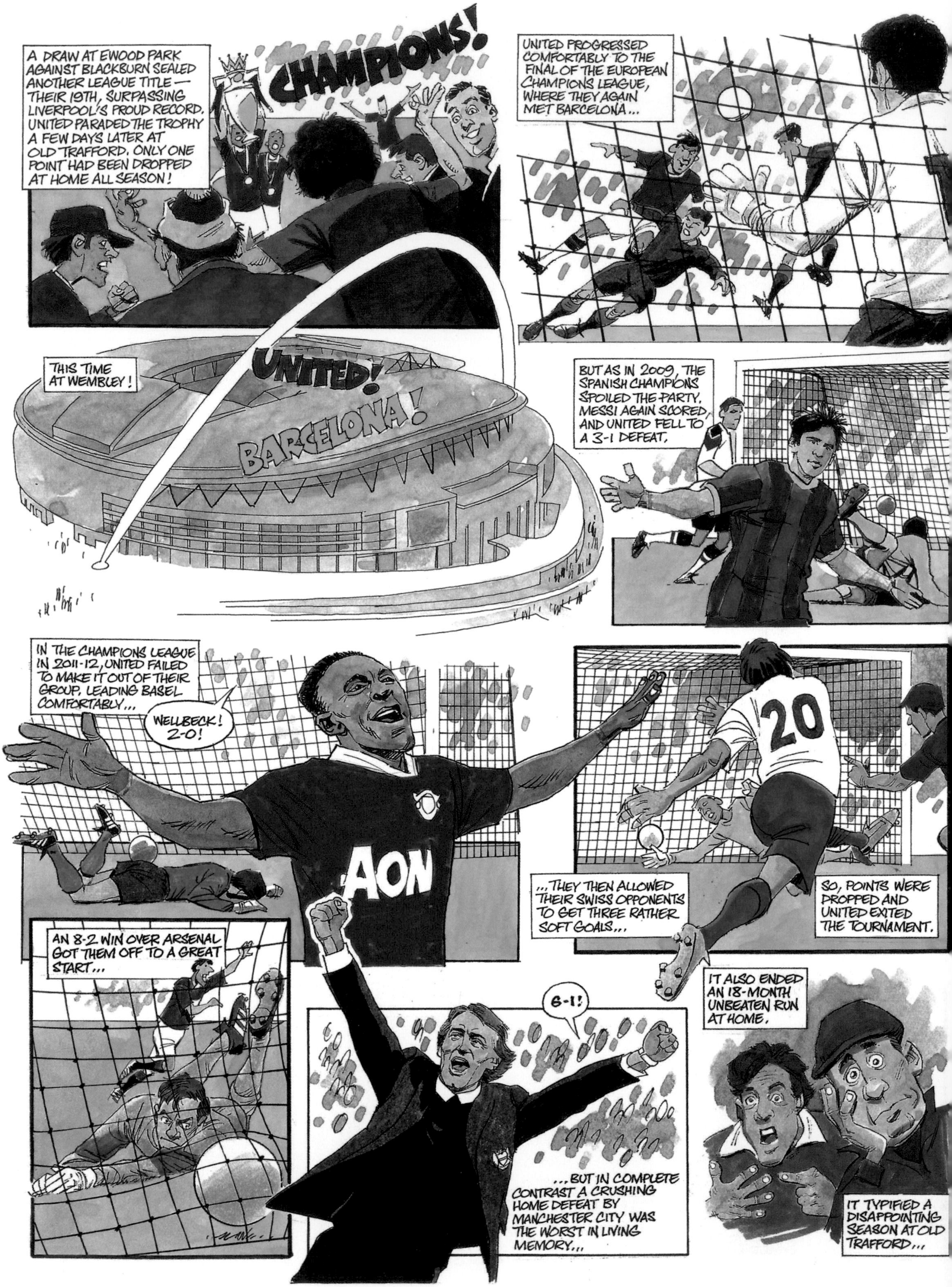
A DRAW AT EWOOD PARK AGAINST BLACKBURN SEALED ANOTHER LEAGUE TITLE — THEIR 19TH, SURPASSING LIVERPOOL'S PROUD RECORD. UNITED PARADED THE TROPHY A FEW DAYS LATER AT OLD TRAFFORD. ONLY ONE POINT HAD BEEN DROPPED AT HOME ALL SEASON!
CHAMPIONS!
UNITED PROGRESSED COMFORTABLY TO THE FINAL OF THE EUROPEAN CHAMPIONS LEAGUE, WHERE THEY AGAIN MET BARCELONA...
THIS TIME AT WEMBLEY!
UNITED!
BARCELONA!
BUT AS IN 2009, THE SPANISH CHAMPIONS SPOILED THE PARTY. MESSI AGAIN SCORED, AND UNITED FELL TO A 3-1 DEFEAT.
IN THE CHAMPIONS LEAGUE IN 2011-12, UNITED FAILED TO MAKE IT OUT OF THEIR GROUP. LEADING BASEL COMFORTABLY...
WELLBECK! 2-0!
AON
20
...THEY THEN ALLOWED THEIR SWISS OPPONENTS TO GET THREE RATHER SOFT GOALS...
SO, POINTS WERE DROPPED AND UNITED EXITED THE TOURNAMENT.
AN 8-2 WIN OVER ARSENAL GOT THEM OFF TO A GREAT START...
6-1!
...BUT IN COMPLETE CONTRAST A CRUSHING HOME DEFEAT BY MANCHESTER CITY WAS THE WORST IN LIVING MEMORY...
IT ALSO ENDED AN 18-MONTH UNBEATEN RUN AT HOME.
IT TYPIFIED A DISAPPOINTING SEASON AT OLD TRAFFORD...

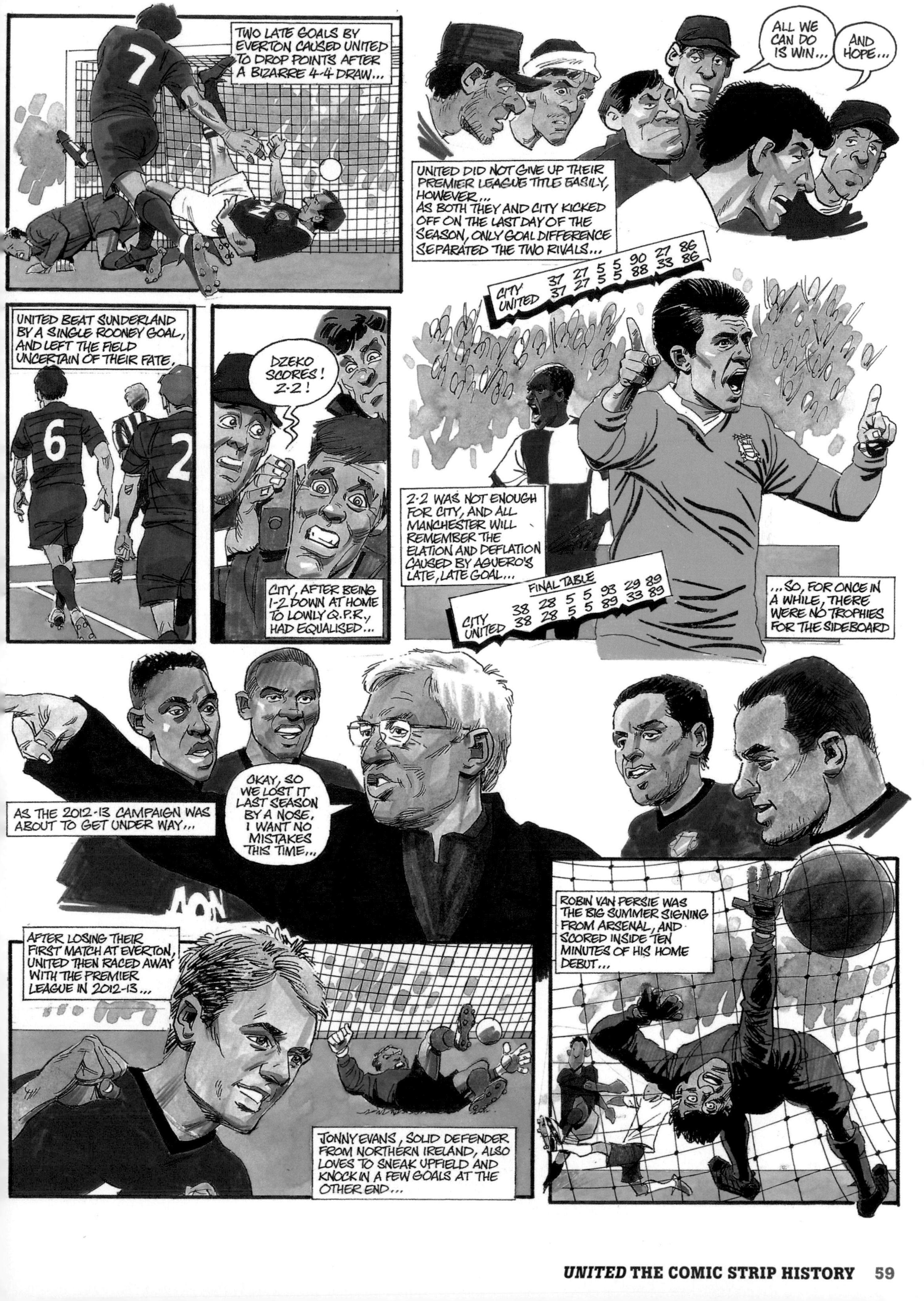

TWO LATE GOALS BY EVERTON CAUSED UNITED TO DROP POINTS AFTER A BIZARRE 4-4 DRAW...
UNITED DID NOT GIVE UP THEIR PREMIER LEAGUE TITLE EASILY, HOWEVER... AS BOTH THEY AND CITY KICKED OFF ON THE LAST DAY OF THE SEASON, ONLY GOAL DIFFERENCE SEPARATED THE TWO RIVALS...
ALL WE CAN DO IS WIN...
AND HOPE...
CITY 37 27 5 5 90 27 86
UNITED 37 27 5 5 88 33 86
UNITED BEAT SUNDERLAND BY A SINGLE ROONEY GOAL, AND LEFT THE FIELD UNCERTAIN OF THEIR FATE.
DZEKO SCORES! 2-2!
CITY, AFTER BEING 1-2 DOWN AT HOME TO LOWLY Q.P.R., HAD EQUALISED...
2-2 WAS NOT ENOUGH FOR CITY, AND ALL MANCHESTER WILL REMEMBER THE ELATION AND DEFLATION CAUSED BY AGUERO'S LATE, LATE GOAL...
FINAL TABLE
CITY 38 28 5 5 93 29 89
UNITED 38 28 5 5 89 33 89
...SO, FOR ONCE IN A WHILE, THERE WERE NO TROPHIES FOR THE SIDEBOARD
AS THE 2012-13 CAMPAIGN WAS ABOUT TO GET UNDER WAY...
OKAY, SO WE LOST IT LAST SEASON BY A NOSE, I WANT NO MISTAKES THIS TIME...
AFTER LOSING THEIR FIRST MATCH AT EVERTON, UNITED THEN RACED AWAY WITH THE PREMIER LEAGUE IN 2012-13...
JONNY EVANS, SOLID DEFENDER FROM NORTHERN IRELAND, ALSO LOVES TO SNEAK UPFIELD AND KNOCK IN A FEW GOALS AT THE OTHER END...
ROBIN VAN PERSIE WAS THE BIG SUMMER SIGNING FROM ARSENAL, AND SCORED INSIDE TEN MINUTES OF HIS HOME DEBUT...

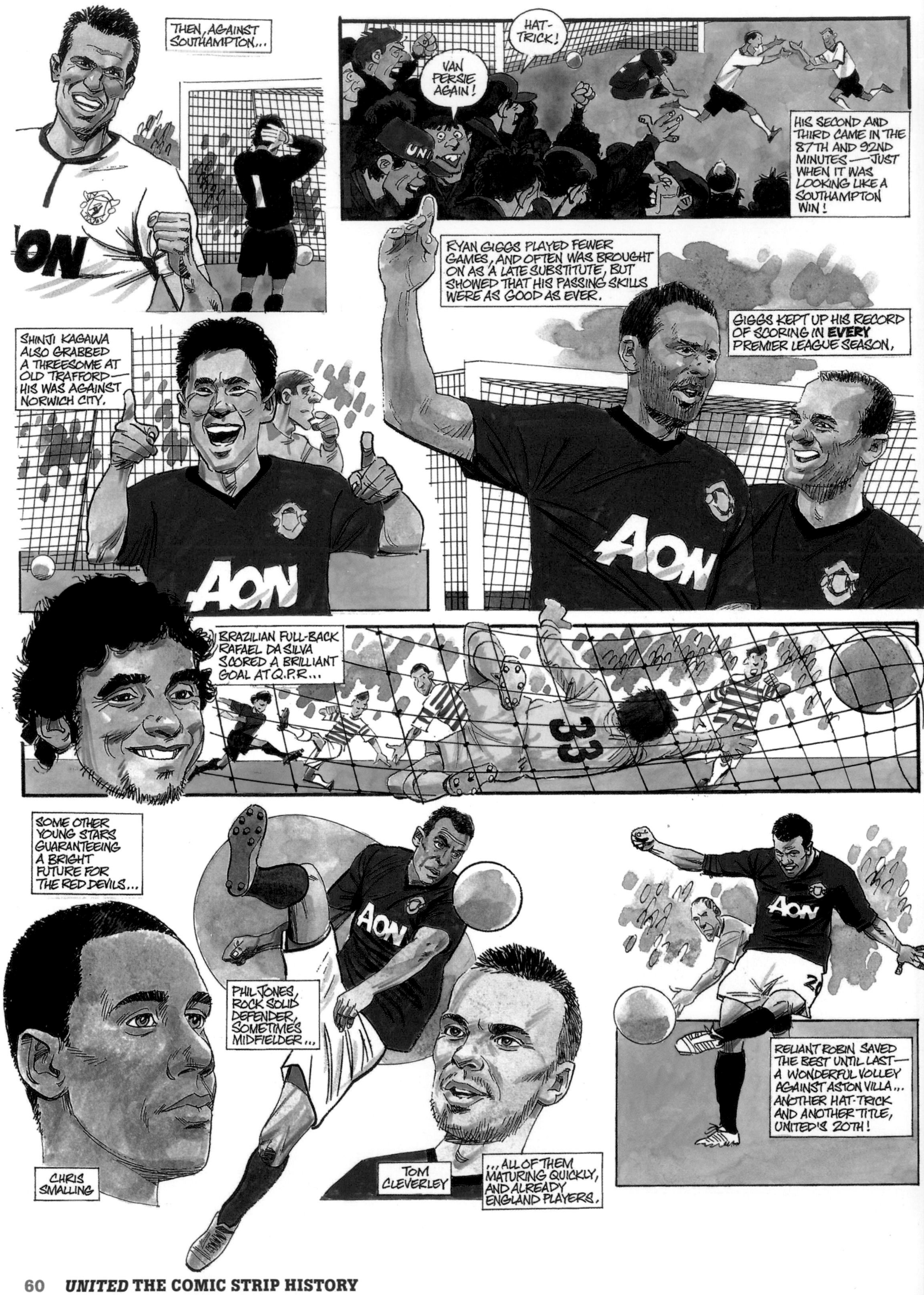
THEN, AGAINST SOUTHAMPTON,..
HAT-TRICK!
VAN PERSIE AGAIN!
HIS SECOND AND THIRD CAME IN THE 87TH AND 92ND MINUTES — JUST WHEN IT WAS LOOKING LIKE A SOUTHAMPTON WIN!
RYAN GIGGS PLAYED FEWER GAMES, AND OFTEN WAS BROUGHT ON AS A LATE SUBSTITUTE, BUT SHOWED THAT HIS PASSING SKILLS WERE AS GOOD AS EVER.
GIGGS KEPT UP HIS RECORD OF SCORING IN **EVERY** PREMIER LEAGUE SEASON.
SHINJI KAGAWA ALSO GRABBED A THREESOME AT OLD TRAFFORD — HIS WAS AGAINST NORWICH CITY.
AON
AON
BRAZILIAN FULL-BACK RAFAEL DA SILVA SCORED A BRILLIANT GOAL AT Q.P.R...
33
SOME OTHER YOUNG STARS GUARANTEEING A BRIGHT FUTURE FOR THE RED DEVILS...
AON
PHIL JONES, ROCK SOLID DEFENDER, SOMETIMES MIDFIELDER...
CHRIS SMALLING
TOM CLEVERLEY
...ALL OF THEM MATURING QUICKLY, AND ALREADY ENGLAND PLAYERS.
AON
RELIANT ROBIN SAVED THE BEST UNTIL LAST — A WONDERFUL VOLLEY AGAINST ASTON VILLA... ANOTHER HAT-TRICK AND ANOTHER TITLE, UNITED'S 20TH!

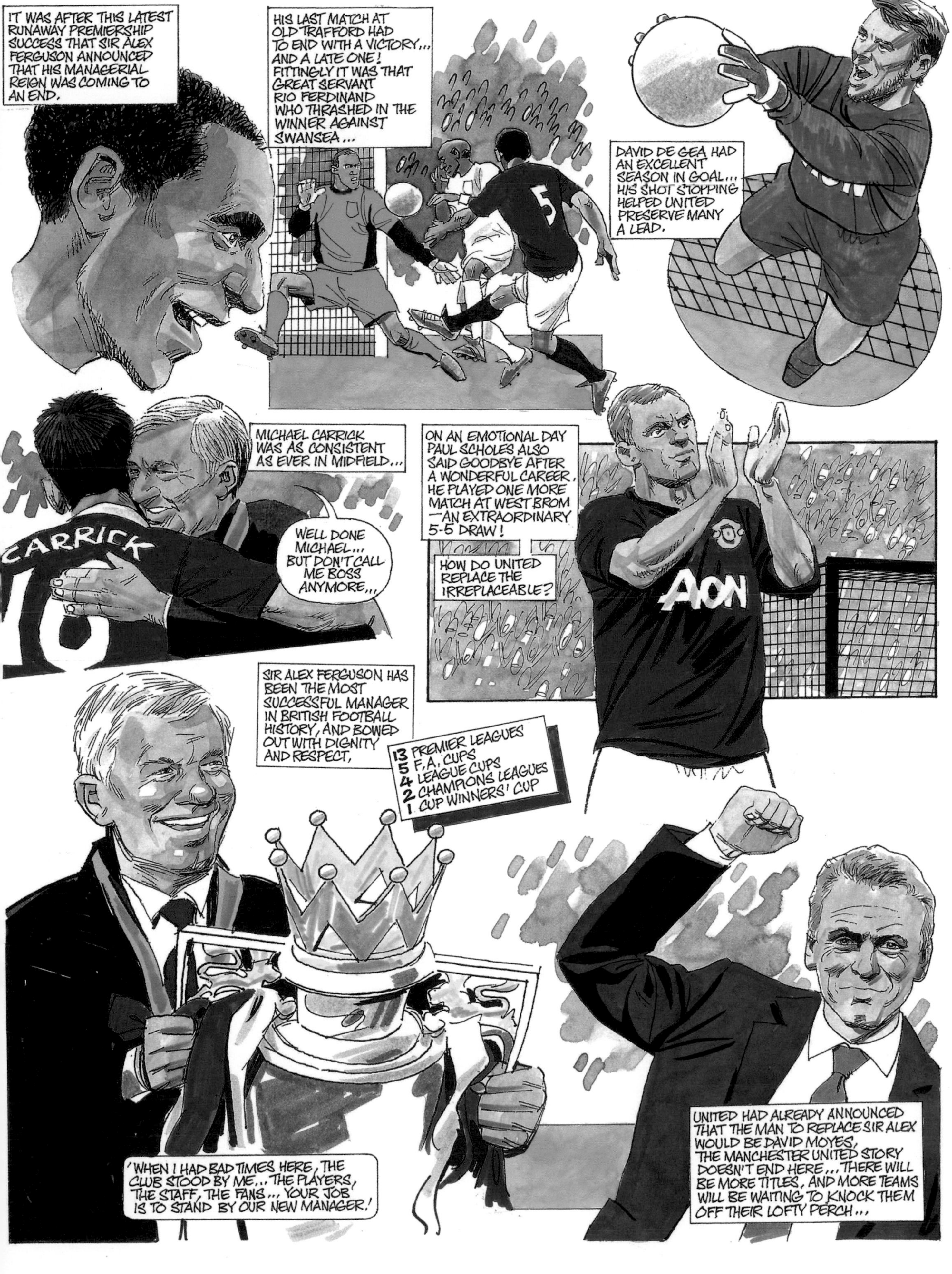
IT WAS AFTER THIS LATEST RUNAWAY PREMIERSHIP SUCCESS THAT SIR ALEX FERGUSON ANNOUNCED THAT HIS MANAGERIAL REIGN WAS COMING TO AN END.
HIS LAST MATCH AT OLD TRAFFORD HAD TO END WITH A VICTORY... AND A LATE ONE! FITTINGLY IT WAS THAT GREAT SERVANT RIO FERDINAND WHO THRASHED IN THE WINNER AGAINST SWANSEA...
5
DAVID DE GEA HAD AN EXCELLENT SEASON IN GOAL... HIS SHOT STOPPING HELPED UNITED PRESERVE MANY A LEAD.
MICHAEL CARRICK WAS AS CONSISTENT AS EVER IN MIDFIELD...
CARRICK
WELL DONE MICHAEL... BUT DON'T CALL ME BOSS ANYMORE...
ON AN EMOTIONAL DAY PAUL SCHOLES ALSO SAID GOODBYE AFTER A WONDERFUL CAREER. HE PLAYED ONE MORE MATCH AT WEST BROM —AN EXTRAORDINARY 5-5 DRAW!
HOW DO UNITED REPLACE THE IRREPLACEABLE?
AON
SIR ALEX FERGUSON HAS BEEN THE MOST SUCCESSFUL MANAGER IN BRITISH FOOTBALL HISTORY, AND BOWED OUT WITH DIGNITY AND RESPECT.
13 PREMIER LEAGUES
5 F.A. CUPS
4 LEAGUE CUPS
2 CHAMPIONS LEAGUES
1 CUP WINNERS' CUP
'WHEN I HAD BAD TIMES HERE, THE CLUB STOOD BY ME... THE PLAYERS, THE STAFF, THE FANS... YOUR JOB IS TO STAND BY OUR NEW MANAGER.'
UNITED HAD ALREADY ANNOUNCED THAT THE MAN TO REPLACE SIR ALEX WOULD BE DAVID MOYES. THE MANCHESTER UNITED STORY DOESN'T END HERE... THERE WILL BE MORE TITLES, AND MORE TEAMS WILL BE WAITING TO KNOCK THEM OFF THEIR LOFTY PERCH...

FACTS & FIGURES

HONOURS

First Division championship: 1907/08, 1910/11, 1951/52, 1955/56, 1956/57, 1964/65, 1966/67

Second Division championship: 1935/36, 1974/75

Premiership: 1992/93, 1993/94, 1995/96, 1996/97, 1998/99, 1999/2000, 2000/01, 2002/03, 2006/07, 2007/08, 2008/09, 2010/11, 2012/13

FA Cup: 1909, 1948, 1963, 1977, 1983, 1985, 1990, 1994, 1996, 1999, 2004

League Cup: 1992, 2006, 2009, 2010

Charity Shield/Community Shield: 1908, 1911, 1952, 1956, 1957, 1965*, 1967*, 1977*, 1983, 1990*, 1993, 1994, 1996, 1997, 2003, 2007, 2008, 2010, 2011* (* joint winners)

European Cup/Champions League: 1968, 1999, 2008

European Cup Winners' Cup: 1991

RECORDS

All-time top appearance makers

1.	Ryan Giggs (1991–)	941
2.	Sir Bobby Charlton (1956–73)	758
3.	Paul Scholes (1994–2013)	718
4.	Bill Foulkes (1952–70)	688
5.	Gary Neville (1992–2011)	608
6.	Alex Stepney (1966–78)	539
7.	Tony Dunne (1960–73)	535
8.	Denis Irwin (1990–2002)	529
9.	Joe Spence (1919–33)	510
10.	Arthur Albiston (1974–88)	485

All-time top goalscorers

1.	Sir Bobby Charlton (1956-73)	249
2.	Denis Law (1962-73)	237
3.	Jack Rowley (1937-55)	211
4.	Wayne Rooney (2008-)	197
5.=	Dennis Viollet (1953-62)	179
5.=	George Best (1963-74)	179
7.=	Joe Spence (1919-33)	168
7.=	Ryan Giggs (1991-)	168
9.	Mark Hughes (1983-86 & 1988-95)	163
10.	Paul Scholes (1994-2013)	150

Record win

10-0 v Anderlecht (h), European Cup preliminary round second leg, 26th September 1956

Record defeat

0-7 v Blackburn Rovers (a), First Division, 10th April 1926

0-7 v Aston Villa (a), First Division, 27th December 1930

0-7 v Wolves (a), First Division, 26th December 1931

Most goals in a match by one player

6 Harold Halse, 25th September 1911, Manchester United 8 Swindon 4 (Charity Shield)

6 George Best, 7th February 1970, Northampton 2 Manchester United 8 (FA Cup 5th rd)

5 Jack Rowley, 12th February 1949, Manchester United 8 Yeovil 0 (FA Cup 5th rd)

5 Andy Cole, 4th March 1995, Manchester United 9 Ipswich 0 (Premiership)

5 Dimitar Berbatov, 27th November 2010, Manchester United 7 Blackburn Rovers 1 (Premiership)

Most Premiership appearances

1.	Ryan Giggs (1991-)	620
2.	Paul Scholes (1994-2013)	499
3.	Gary Neville (1992-2011)	400

Most Premiership goals

1.	Wayne Rooney (2008-)	141
2.	Ryan Giggs (1991-)	109
3.	Paul Scholes (1994-2013)	107
4.	Ruud van Nistelrooy (2001-06)	95
5.	Andy Cole (1995-2001)	93

Most goals in Europe

1.	Ruud van Nistelrooy (2001-06)	38
2.	Wayne Rooney (2008-)	31
3.	Ryan Giggs (1991-)	29
4.	Denis Law (1962-73)	28
5.	Paul Scholes (1994-2013)	26

Most FA Cup goals

1.	Denis Law (1962-73)	34
2.	Jack Rowley (1937-55)	26
3.	George Best (1963-74)	21
4.	Stan Pearson (1937-54)	21
5.	Bobby Charlton (1956-73)	19

Record home attendances

82,771*, 29th January 1949, Manchester United 1 Bradford Park Avenue 1 (FA Cup 4th rd)

81,962*, 17th January 1948, Manchester United 1 Arsenal 1 (Division One)

81,565*, 12th February 1949, Manchester United 8 Yeovil 0 (FA Cup 5th rd)

76,098, 31st March 2007, Manchester United 4 Blackburn 1 (Premiership)

76,073, 13th January 2007, Manchester United 3 Aston Villa 1 (Premiership)

* Home matches played at Maine Road following wartime bomb damage to Old Trafford

Most substitute appearances

1.	Ryan Giggs (1991-)	154
2.	Ole Gunnar Solskjaer (1996-2007)	150
3.	Paul Scholes (1994-2013)	141
4.	John O'Shea (1999-2011)	92
5.	Phil Neville (1995-2005)	85

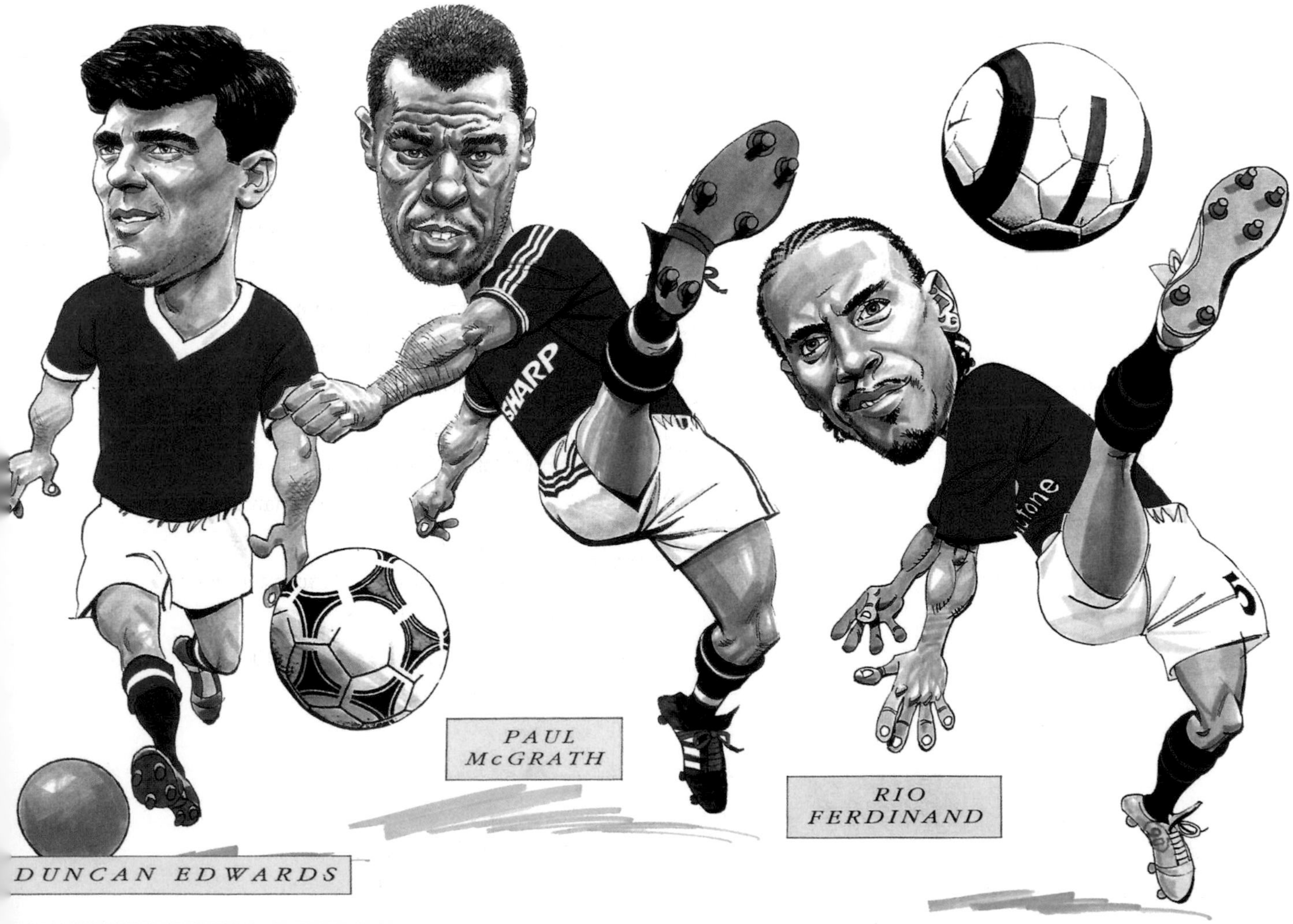
SHARP
PAUL McGRATH
RIO FERDINAND
DUNCAN EDWARDS

Published by Vision Sports Publishing Limited in 2013

Vision Sports Publishing Ltd
19-23 High Street
Kingston upon Thames
Surrey
KT1 1LL
www.visionsp.co.uk

ISBN: 978-1909534-14-8

This book is 100 per cent unofficial

Art and script: Bob Bond
Cover artwork: Stephen Gulbis
Cover design: Neal Cobourne
Editor: Jim Drewett
Production Editor: John Murray

Printed in China by Hung Hing

A CIP Catalogue record for this book is available from the British Library

BOB BOND
Caricatures of many of the legendary United players drawn by this book's
illustrator, Bob Bond, can be purchased, as postcards or A3 and A4 prints.
Email **bobbond@live.co.uk** for a list of players available. Excellent as gift ideas,
for autographing, or to add to your personal memorabilia collection.

STEPHEN GULBIS
Football and art prints by Stephen Gulbis are available from **www.thefootballartist.com**